Hunting Practices of the Wachiperi

Demystifying Indigenous Environmental Behavior

Rodolfo Tello

Library of Congress Control Number: 2013900855

ISBN-10: 148-195-085-1
ISBN-13: 978-148-195-085-5

Cover Design: Línea Digital SAC
www.lineadigital.com

Jaguar cover photograph: Kyslynskyy / Fotolia

CreateSpace Publishing
4900 LaCross Road
North Charleston, SC 29406
www.createspace.com

Printed in the United States of America

TABLE OF CONTENTS

TABLES AND FIGURES

Tables

Figures

Introduction

In July 2008, the leader of the Wachiperi community of Queros signed a contract with the Peruvian government to manage a conservation concession for a renewable period of forty years. This event was the result of a collaborative partnership between an indigenous community and an environmental organization, which provided people from Queros with the required technical and financial support to embark on this initiative. The adoption of environmental protection activities by the Wachiperi was an indication of the active engagement of this indigenous community in natural resource conservation. However, this was not always the case. In the lapse of a few decades there were times when they displayed a pattern characterized by harvesting activities directly leading to the degradation of the environment. As such, the community of Queros is an excellent example of the variation through time of indigenous environmental behavior.

The analysis of the environmental behavior of the Wachiperi provides insights into the relationship between indigenous peoples and biodiversity in tropical forests, which is a highly controversial topic. Some view indigenous peoples as "natural" conservationists whose ecologically friendly lifestyle is an example of sustainable livelihoods (Clay 1988; Warren 2001). However, others see them as a growing threat to the conservation of tropical biodiversity (Terborgh 2000; Redford and Sanderson 2000). A third group of authors perceive them as "adaptive" agents whose environmental behavior depends on their specific local conditions (Berkes

1

2004: 626; Balée and Erickson 2006). The latter approach does not assume intrinsic behaviors and focuses instead on the analysis of the factors that encourage indigenous groups either to pursue sustainable livelihoods or to adopt practices leading to environmental degradation.

The impact of indigenous peoples on tropical biodiversity through animal hunting has been a key area of discussion. To contribute to this debate, the main question explored in this book is: What explains the variation in the levels of hunting intensity among the Wachiperi? More specific questions include (1) To what extent do regional historical processes help explain the current intensity of hunting? (2) How has the social division of labor shaped their hunting practices? (3) How important are cross-cultural factors in the establishment of their present levels of hunting? (4) What are the most significant factors influencing their current levels of hunting? And (5) what are the implications of changes in the intensity of hunting for both biodiversity and the living conditions of the Wachiperi? In a context where indigenous ways of life are greatly influenced by environmental policies and practices informed by preconceived notions, this book fills a gap in empirical knowledge about the environmental behavior of indigenous peoples and provides methodological guidance to elucidate this process.

Field research for this study was conducted among the Wachiperi of Queros, an indigenous[1] community in the southwestern part of the Peruvian rain forest (see Figure 1). Queros is located within the Kosñipata district of the province of Paucartambo, in the Cusco region.

---

[1] The term "indigenous" refers to a socially constructed category based on self-identification, linked to aspects like ancestry, history, territoriality, linguistic and cultural expressions, and positionality in relation to non-indigenous persons. This term is not intended to describe an immutable attribute, since the changes in their way of life constantly redefine what it means to be indigenous. Moreover, the use of the term "indigenous" in this book basically refers to groups in the Amazon region experiencing similar situations as the Wachiperi. The terms "indigenous communities," "indigenous groups," "indigenous peoples," and "indigenous population" are all used interchangeably.

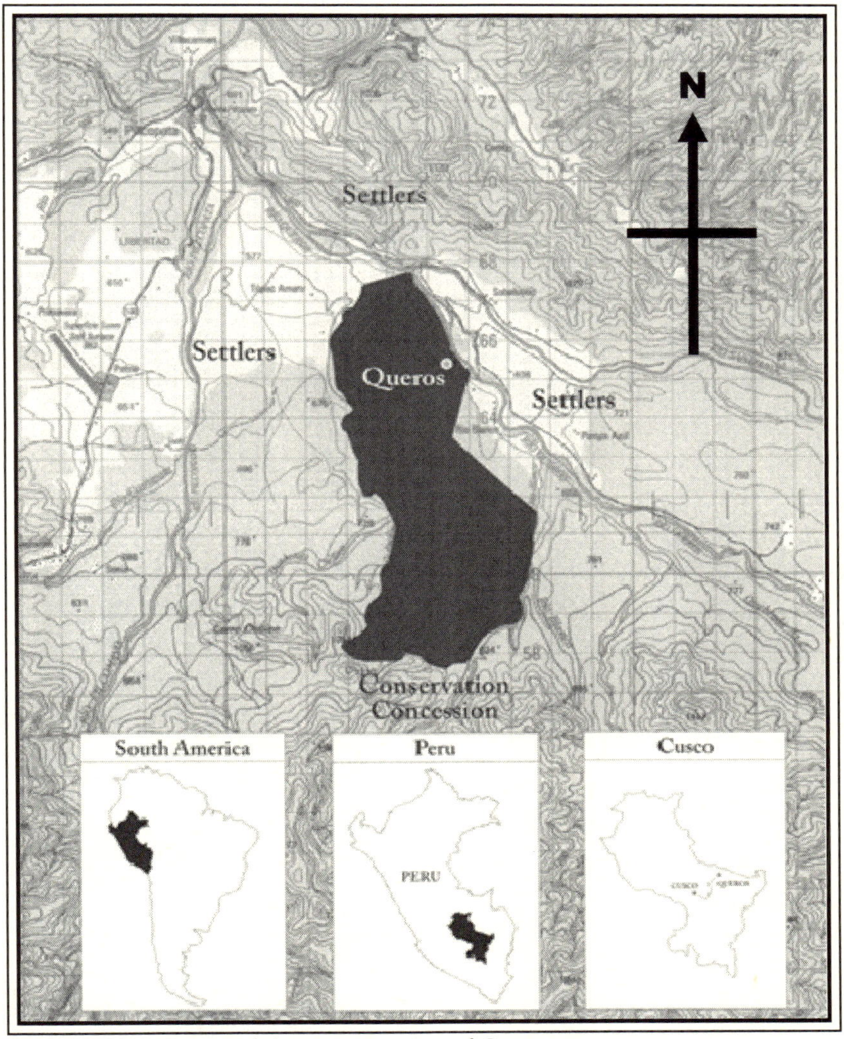

Figure 1. Location of the community of Queros
Source: Instituto Geográfico Nacional &
         Asociación para la Conservación de la
         Cuenca Amazónica.

The community of Queros is situated in the Amazonian multiple use zone of Manu National Park, a place with one of the highest concentrations of biodiversity on earth (Terborgh 2004: 23). The weather in the area near Queros is warm and humid, with abundant rain throughout the year, especially between November and March.

The Wachiperi have lived in the Kosñipata Valley for about a thousand years (Llosa and Nieto 2003). They alternated periods of conflict with periods of peace with other indigenous groups of the region, the Incas, and the Spaniards. Beginning in the middle of the sixteenth century, the Spaniards established agricultural plantations in the area, exchanging products with the Wachiperi in times of peace (Califano 1985). Despite occasional exchanges with their neighbors, the Wachiperi did not establish permanent relationships with members of Western society until the middle of the twentieth century, at which time these exchanges with outsiders brought about the transmission of external diseases, particularly smallpox, which killed approximately 65% of the Wachiperi population (Pinasco 2002: 13). These massive deaths affected the Wachiperi in dramatic ways. Under these circumstances, they had no choice but to resettle in a Baptist mission that had recently been established in the area. The missionaries had invited the Wachiperi to live there and offered additional support, including medical attention, for the remaining survivors. This relocation was a major event for the Wachiperi, who in the span of a few years saw their lives deeply transformed. However, the fact that the Wachiperi maintained a relatively independent way of life until the 1950s placed them in a different position from most groups in the Amazon region, who, for the most part, were severely disrupted by the effects of colonization since the earlier stages of Spanish occupation in the sixteenth century (Lathrap 1973).

The establishment of closer relationships between the Wachiperi and members of Western society created significant changes in their livelihoods. Shortly after moving into the Baptist mission, the Wachiperi adopted market-oriented activities in addition to their customary practices of subsistence. Their interactions with missionaries, along with the increasing number of settlers coming to the Kosñipata Valley in the following decades, created significant changes in the Wachiperi lifestyle, posing a constant challenge for them to find ways to combine their expectations for environmental conservation and socioeconomic development.[2] Conserving the local forests is important for their subsistence, as is their growing need for market products that were gradually introduced into their way of life. As a result of these changes, some activities, such as hunting, have experienced a significant reduction in the last five decades. Other activities have experienced an expansion, like agriculture, as large part of the community's agricultural production is now intended for sale in Pillcopata, a nearby town and the political capital of the Kosñipata district. Pillcopata is mostly inhabited by former Andean settlers who came to the area about three decades ago.

The current population in Queros is approximately sixty people, which represents only a small fraction of the historical Wachiperi population before the middle of the twentieth century. People from Queros frequently visit the town of Pillcopata, where they have relatives and friends. Some members of the community of Queros even live in Pillcopata on a full-time basis but are still affiliated with the Queros indigenous community. Accordingly, the community of Queros should be understood not as a territorially bounded village, but mainly as a network of people whose activities transcend a single physical location.

Pillcopata is located about seven miles away from Queros. A dirt road connects Queros to Pillcopata. Queros

---

[2] The term "development" is understood as the pursuit of improvements in the living conditions of a population based on their own criteria. This approach is related to the idea of "community-driven development," which refers to processes where "community groups initiate, organize, and take action to achieve common interests and goals" (Narayan 1998: 103), as well as to the idea of "ethnodevelopment," which refers to the "sense of ethnic identity, close attachment to ancestral land, and capacity to mobilize labor, capital, and other resources for shared goals" (Van Nieuwkoop and Uquillas 2000: 3).

residents make frequent trips to Pillcopata in about two hours on foot. Buses run three times a week from Pillcopata to Cusco, the closest city in the region, and the trip takes about nine hours. Although Queros is the community where most Wachiperi are currently concentrated, some Wachiperi families live in other indigenous communities. People from Queros estimate the total current Wachiperi population at about ninety individuals. However, for practical reasons, mention of the Wachiperi in this study is limited only to people belonging to this indigenous group who are current members of Queros.

Regarding the environmental behavior of the Wachiperi, an examination of the changes in their hunting practices is important because hunting used to be critical to their subsistence in the ancestral way of life. Traditionally, hunting was conducted mostly by men, but women also played an important role in butchering, distributing, and cooking meat, and also in influencing hunters' decision-making processes, such as convincing them to go hunting. Women also contributed agricultural goods and other products gathered in the forest, playing a critical role in the group's subsistence. Today, the intensity of hunting in Queros is significantly lower than the hunting levels around the middle of the twentieth century. Their current harvest of meat is for subsistence, to celebrate festivities in the community, for recreational purposes, and to prepare meals for their guests. The main animals hunted are small and medium-sized terrestrial mammals like armadillos, peccaries, tapirs, pacas, deer, and capybaras. Birds are also hunted on a regular basis, including spix's guan, white-throated tinamou, and common piping guan. In addition to hunting, other activities include agriculture, logging, gathering, fishing, raising chickens, tourism, conservation, and working as salaried employees.

The community of Queros was selected as the research site because at the time I was looking for a place to conduct my research, people in Queros were engaging in novel processes that were different from the ancestral practices of subsistence commonly associated with indigenous communities. These new processes included negotiations with the Peruvian government to allow the Wachiperi to manage a conservation concession, the establishment of a partnership with a regional environmental organization, their engagement in community-based tourism activities, and struggles with settlers and the mayor of Pillcopata over the use of the land in areas adjacent to their community. The existence of community members with a college education who were working on these projects was another relevant factor that stimulated my interest in finding out the extent to which higher education made a difference in that community. Also influential in the selection of Queros as my research site was my previous experience working with this community as a coordinator of indigenous affairs on a sustainable development project. This experience provided me with background knowledge about their social and environmental behavior and allowed me to recognize the importance of the recent changes in their lifestyle.

In relation to the analytical approach adopted in this study, unlike positions that perceive indigenous peoples as natural conservationists (Clay 1988: 4; Posey 1998: 115; Warren 2001: 453; Meggers 1971: 2) or as threats to tropical biodiversity (Terborgh 2000: 1359; Redford and Sanderson 2000: 1362; Robinson et al. 1999: 595; Oates 2000: B6), my research is based on an approach that understands indigenous peoples as adaptive agents whose environmental behavior varies according to their specific conditions (Balée and Erickson 2006: 12; Chicchon 1993: 15; Berkes and Folke 1998: 10). To analyze the factors that encourage indigenous communities to either pursue sustainable livelihoods or to adopt practices leading to environmental degradation, I included elements from a wide body of anthropological and interdisciplinary literature. Scholarly publications identified different factors affecting indigenous environmental behavior in tropical forests and attempted to explain what causes its variation in different geographical, cultural, and temporal scenarios. I have grouped these contributions into biological models, socioeconomic approaches, and cultural explanations, along with the historical processes associated with particular research settings.

My way of addressing this general body of literature is to acknowledge that all the factors identified as influential in indigenous environmental behavior may be important in some cases but not in others. Yet how the relevance of each potentially influential factor varies from one setting to another has for the most part not been considered, which required adopting an approach based on a more flexible understanding of the issues surrounding hunting intensity. During the review of the literature, I searched for an analytical framework capable of (1) exploring the potential of multiple factors identified as influential in other geographical and cultural contexts, (2) allowing for the identification of the most relevant factors influencing hunting intensity and the way they interact in each particular research setting, and (3) articulating different levels of analysis in the examination of the interplay between multiple influential factors and a historical perspective. Such an approach was provided by the ethnographic application of the root cause analysis methodology (Steadman-Edwards 1998; Wood et al. 2000). Root causes analysis offers the means to identify and differentiate between the root causes and the proximate causes of variation in environmental outcomes and processes. Root cause analysis also provides a high level of flexibility when identifying the most influential aspects of environmental behavior, according to the empirical conditions of each research setting. Based on this approach, I examined the different factors that the literature identified as influential, and evaluated their empirical relevance in the case of the Wachiperi, within the context of the historical processes associated with this particular group.

While conducting this study, I found that one of the most directly influential factors leading to the decline in hunting intensity among the Wachiperi has been the diversification of their livelihoods in the context of a mixed economy, which mainly refers to the inclusion of income-generating activities in addition to their subsistence practices. Livelihood diversification is a proximate cause promoted by a series of cultural and ecological changes resulting from the increased interactions the Wachiperi had to establish with outsiders since the middle of the twentieth century. In turn, these changes were shaped by larger socioeconomic forces in their historical experience that affected their social and environmental conditions. Particularly relevant were the deep social disruptions created after most Wachiperi died, leaving them with no choice but to establish even closer relationships with members of Western society, and their transition from a subsistence economy to a mixed economy. While these conditions are, in principle, only valid in the case of the Wachiperi, the existence of similar conditions among other indigenous groups (cf. Lu 2007; Tucker 2001), particularly the transition from a subsistence economy toward a mixed economy as a result of the expansion of the global economy, suggests the need to include the approach of this study into current understandings of indigenous environmental behavior in other settings as well.[3]

In the context of this research, hunting intensity is understood as an operational term that indicates the level of pressure on forest animals created by the hunting practices of the Wachiperi. At the level of indicators, it is mainly defined by the frequency of hunting and the number of animals hunted. However, in practice, the lack of baseline information about these variables in the past did not allow for direct comparisons. Instead, I relied on reconstructions based on the collective perceptions of the Wachiperi about both the intensity of their hunting practices in different historical moments and the identification of trends in their hunting behavior. Accordingly, variation in hunting intensity among the Wachiperi is understood based on a comparison of two roughly defined

---

[3] The potential application of the lessons from this study in different circumstances should be analyzed in each case, since it may or may not be relevant in other settings. That determination should be a matter of empirical analysis to evaluate its applicability. Accordingly, the reference made about other indigenous peoples is intended for groups living in tropical rain forests and experiencing similar conditions as the Wachiperi, such as having a sedentary life, access to community lands, and a combination of subsistence practices and income-generating activities, characteristic of a mixed economy.

periods in time. The first period is located around the middle of the twentieth century, when the intensity of hunting was relatively high and the way of life of the indigenous population was less affected by Western ideas and practices than it is today. The second period refers to the beginning of the twenty-first century, when the intensity of hunting is relatively low and the people in the community have been affected by a greater degree of Western influence than around the middle of the twentieth century. In addition, this analysis also includes the fluctuating variation in the levels of hunting intensity produced between these two periods.

Diversification of livelihoods is another key factor, which refers to the process in which people "construct an increasingly diverse portfolio of activities and assets in order to survive and to improve their standards of living" (Ellis 2000: 15). Livelihood diversification implies the existence of alternative socioeconomic activities coexisting with hunting. As part of this diversification process, people allocate their scarce productive resources among the available alternatives, according to their level of contribution toward the satisfaction of people's changing needs and desires. The influence of alternative socioeconomic activities on indigenous environmental behavior has been explored by a number of scholars in different contexts, including the investment of more time in agriculture and wage labor and less in hunting activities (Vickers 1994: 307), the substitution of fish for game as an alternative source of protein (Ohl et al. 2008: 838), the intensification of hunting to ensure food provision in response to uncertain agricultural harvests (Tucker 2006: 22), and the introduction of locally viable forms of income generation as an alternative to hunting (Hofer et al. 1996: 142), among others.

An important related concept is mixed economy, which refers to the coexistence of subsistence practices and income-generating activities with similar degrees of relevance in the livelihoods of indigenous groups. The idea of a mixed economy is based on the recognition that indigenous groups sometimes practice a "mix of activities" that produces different configurations (Tucker 2007: 162). Likewise, in situations where indigenous groups engage in market activities, as Lu has pointed out, "It cannot be assumed that once indigenous peoples participate in the market, they forsake subsistence practices and thus lose their connection with the natural environment" but instead become the creators of "mixed" or "hybrid" economies (Lu 2007: 601). This idea is consistent with my assessment of the process experienced by the Wachiperi.

Regarding the use of the term "conservation," in a broad sense it refers to people's collective responsibility of "caring for the earth and its inhabitants, human and other" (Little 1999: 275), especially when intentional actions are designed to prevent or mitigate environmental degradation (Smith and Wishnie 2000: 493). However, this term is often used in different ways, each of them concealing various political ideas. As David Harvey has pointed out, there is a wide political diversity among the existing positions and discourses about the environment. These positions are presented in a way that avoids disclosing their political assumptions, but each of them has its own combination of beliefs, practices, institutions, organization, and power relations that shape their usage (Harvey 1996: 177–180). For the purposes of this study, I found it useful to differentiate between three types of conservation actions, each of them reflecting a distinctive political background, even though in some cases they present significant degrees of overlapping. The first type, "mainstream conservation" (cf. Colchester 1994: 57), refers to environmental projects designed or carried out by multilateral institutions, government agencies, and international environmental organizations and their national implementing partners. The second type is "grassroots conservation" (Hall 1997), also known as "environmentalism of the poor" (Martinez-Alier 2002: 10), which is based on actions aimed at protecting the environment at the local level. The third type, "community-based conservation," refers to grassroots conservation initiatives that incorporate the potential of collaboration with mainstream conservation institutions, linking efforts at both levels previously mentioned to achieve greater effectiveness in natural resource management, and assuming conservation and development as complementary parts of integrated strategies (Russell and Harshbarger 2003: 21). In the case of the Wachiperi, their recent actions fall mostly within the third type.

I first arrived in the community of Queros in the middle of 2002, as part of my involvement as a coordinator of indigenous affairs in Pro-Manu, a sustainable development project funded by both the European Union and the Peruvian government. Until the end of 2004, this experience allowed me to conduct research and frequently interact with people in the community, especially conducting informal interviews about their way of life. My main tasks were to support the planning process of an ecotourism initiative of the community and update its environmental management plan. I also conducted research for a booklet publication about culture and environment in the community of Queros (Tello 2004), and a social assessment of the potential impacts of a small electrification project for this community. More recently, I spent time between 2008 and 2009 researching the hunting practices of the Wachiperi.

As a predominantly qualitative research enterprise, my main method for the collection of ethnographic data during the time I spent in the community of Queros was participant observation, including the recording of ethnographic research notes. Participant observation about the different activities conducted by the Wachiperi was useful for both data collection and data analysis, since it provided a way to understand explicit and implicit aspects of the local culture.

I also interviewed many people from Queros, settlers living in Pillcopata and the surrounding areas of Queros, and also people external to the community. With the Wachiperi living in Queros and Pillcopata, I conducted semi-structured interviews, and interviewed many participants on more than one occasion. These interviews included men and women, members of different age groups, and individuals with different levels of exposure to Western culture. The interviews were conducted in Spanish, which to varying degrees is spoken by every person in Queros. I also benefited from the help of a research assistant from the community, who helped me coordinate the interviews and assisted me with occasional translations. Likewise, I interviewed settlers currently living in Pillcopata and other places near the community of Queros, seeking a greater understanding of their own hunting activities and their perceptions about Wachiperi hunting practices. Other people I interviewed include a Wachiperi healer and spiritual leader living in a different indigenous community, a plantation owner who lived close to Pillcopata, and a Baptist missionary who worked with the Wachiperi in the 1960s.

In addition to these interviews, I also conducted two surveys about the hunting practices of people from Queros that covered almost two-thirds of the adult members of the community, both men and women. The first survey was conducted in 2008 and the second one in 2009. These surveys helped me identify general hunting patterns, develop a sense of proportion about them, collect systematic data about people's attitudes and opinions, and assess the distribution of their answers. I also constructed a census, which gave me a sense of demographic distribution, conjugal practices and residence patterns, and created maps of the area that provided graphic representations of their living space. I also took photographs to provide a visual illustration of contemporary activities.

The process of analyzing the ethnographic data gathered was informed by several activities. Participant observation led me to increasingly make sense of the empirical information collected, as a task that involved observing things and asking questions. The analysis of the information from both the field observations recorded in my ethnographic notebooks and the interviews I conducted was facilitated by the use of a tagging system. This system was based on the factors identified as potentially influential during the literature review and the ones identified during fieldwork, which allowed me to assess the extent to which factors addressed as influential in other cultural and geographical settings were relevant in the case of the Wachiperi.

During the last stage of my research, the interactive nature of the interviews provided me with a space to try out some preliminary interpretations on the ground and adjust them based on feedback provided by the Wachiperi. The information from the surveys and census was entered into electronic databases, allowing the identification and visualization of statistical patterns. The use of descriptive statistics was important in providing a sense of proportion among the different variables, as well as in assessing the internal variability of hunting practices and perceptions among the Wachiperi. The information gathered through the use of several techniques of data analysis was triangulated and interpreted in relation to one another.

The methodological approach adopted in this book can be best described as the ethnographic application of the root cause analysis framework (Stedman-Edwards 1998; Wood et al. 2000), which allowed me to integrate different types of data in a coherent way. For instance, diversification of livelihoods was addressed as a proximate cause, influenced by intermediate causes like cultural and ecological changes. Each of these factors was addressed both in terms of its own influence on hunting and in relation to one another, examining the effect of their combined interactions. This method of analysis also allowed me to assess the empirical relevance of different influential factors in explaining the variation of Wachiperi hunting practices. During the analysis process, I gave precedence to the use of empirical information over the use of predefined ideas about social and environmental factors.

Based on these considerations, this study provides analytical insights into the empirical conditions underlying the relationship between indigenous peoples and tropical biodiversity, which I believe are not limited to the case of the Wachiperi but could be useful in other settings as well. I share my findings in this study, addressing crucial issues for members, friends, and allies of indigenous communities; applied environmental anthropologists; conservation social scientists; interdisciplinary practitioners; and people interested in conserving biodiversity in tropical rain forests in general, particularly those involved in the design and implementation of conservation policies and strategies.

This study is organized into five chapters. Chapter One examines how the historical experiences of the Wachiperi have helped shape their specific social and environmental conditions, identifying the particularities of this indigenous group based on their own processes and events. A brief description of the customary way of life of the Wachiperi around the middle of the twentieth century provides important historical information to understand their recent process of socioeconomic and cultural change. Particularly relevant is the increased interaction of the Wachiperi with members of Western society in the second half of the twentieth century, which created profound disruptions in their living conditions. The chapter concludes with an analysis of the extent to which the most relevant processes and events in their recent history have influenced their current levels of hunting intensity.

Chapter Two addresses the relevance of gender roles in the hunting practices of the Wachiperi through an analysis of their social division of labor. The productive activities of people in Queros are briefly discussed, focusing on men's and women's participation in each activity since the middle of the twentieth century. Special attention is paid to hunting and the role played by women in this activity, since women's influence on hunting has, for the most part, been excluded from ethnographic accounts. In addition to hunting, this chapter describes other subsistence practices like agriculture, fishing, gathering, and household chores, among others.

Chapter Three is a succinct exploration of how diverse factors affecting hunting intensity among indigenous peoples in different places and cultures are relevant in the case of the Wachiperi. These factors include a series of material conditions, cultural attitudes, and structural processes identified as relevant in the literature review. The chapter identifies the diversification of livelihoods as the most directly influential empirical factor contributing to the current levels of hunting intensity among the Wachiperi, based on its recurrence across the different areas examined.

Chapter Four addresses the influence of livelihood diversification on the levels of hunting intensity among the Wachiperi, particularly in the last decade. It includes a section on the increasing adoption of commercial activities in their productive practices, especially agriculture and logging, and a section on sustainable enterprises, such as community-based tourism and environmental conservation. The chapter ends with a discussion about the current expectations of the Wachiperi about improvements in their living conditions, especially regarding the need to conduct both subsistence and market-oriented activities as part of their mixed economy.

Chapter Five describes the most relevant social trends influencing Wachiperi hunting practices. It includes a section on the process of cultural change that has been taking place since the middle of the twentieth century, and a section about the greater interaction between the people of Queros and outsiders in the last decade. The examination of these processes complements the previous chapter by illustrating how larger social dynamics have been shaping the diversification of indigenous livelihoods, and by linking this specific factor affecting hunting intensity with other elements on a broader level of analysis. The chapter ends with a discussion about the need to incorporate these recent trends into our understanding of the current environmental behavior of the Wachiperi and similar indigenous groups inhabiting tropical rain forests.

The findings of this book are presented in a conclusions section, where I summarize the main aspects covered in the different chapters and organize them according to the research questions posed in the introduction. I also present some recommendations based on the experience of the Wachiperi.

The chapters are intended to be read in the order they appear, since they follow a logical sequence in which each chapter builds on the previous one. The temporal focus also moves forward with each chapter. While all the chapters illustrate a different dimension of the main research question explored, the first chapters focus on the middle of the twentieth century, while the last chapters focus on processes that have become particularly influential in the last decades. Likewise, these chapters should not be considered as standalone documents, since understanding the complex interactions surrounding indigenous environmental behavior requires maintaining a sense of interconnectedness between the multiple aspects discussed in the chapters, which together provide an explanation of the topic under consideration.

I would like to express my gratitude to the members of the community of Queros, including Walter Quertehuari, Nelly Ninantay, Maruja Yonaje, and Julian Dariquebe. I am also thankful to many other people who helped me undertake this writing project, particularly David Vine, Brett Williams, Bryan McNeil, Dolores Koenig, Michael Mascia, Molly Mimier, Luciano Bornholdt, and members of my family. I also owe my thanks to funding sources like the Robyn Rafferty Mathias Fund and the Cosmos Club Foundation. Staff of the Amazon Conservation Association and the Manu National Park administration was also extremely helpful in this process.

Chapter I

Socioeconomic Transitions in History

When it comes to displaying emotions, the Wachiperi are not a particularly expressive group of people. However, there were occasions when I could tell they were experiencing deep feelings, such as when sharing unhappy memories. During a visit of tourists to Queros in 2009, the tour guide from the community made a stop at a place where a now-closed Baptist mission was once located. The tour guide mentioned that he and other Wachiperi were born there and explained how they lived in the 1960s, and how that land is now controlled by settlers. When speaking, his eyes fixed on nothing in particular. His tone of voice became steadier, seeming to detach himself from the story but suggesting deep underlying feelings. This attitude was also found in other accounts of the Wachiperi about their historical experience, particularly when they talked about the hardships they endured in the years following the establishment of permanent relationships with Western society, the massive deaths as a result of the introduction of illnesses such as smallpox, and the current occupation of their ancestral lands by outsiders. As painful as it was, the Wachiperi wanted their history to be known by their friends, guests, and allies. Recounting events from the past seemed to create an anchor that strengthened the links of the Wachiperi with their collective memory. It also served as a source of reflection when exploring new avenues for the future, adapting their behavior according to what they feel is right in a world that is constantly changing.

This chapter provides a succinct description of the most relevant historical processes and events experienced by the Wachiperi, which provides a foundation for understanding subsequent chapters, since many aspects of their current hunting practices have been influenced by historical factors. Accordingly, addressing the past is a critical step toward a holistic and multidimensional approach. The relevance of a historical analysis becomes even clearer when considering that some factors identified here as influential in hunting are also consistent with the findings of subsequent chapters, displaying internal coherence and providing mutual reinforcement.

The data presented here is organized around the most relevant periods to the historical experience of the Wachiperi, which include the Pre-Hispanic (before 1531), Colonial (1532–1820), Republican (1821–1949) and Post-Contact (1950–present) periods. This chapter ends with a discussion about the extent to which the historical experience of the Wachiperi, particularly the establishment of closer relationships with members of Western society, has influenced the intensity of their current hunting practices.

The Time of Hinkiori

The Wachiperi have inhabited the Kosñipata Valley since ancient times. Llosa and Nieto explained that groups like the Wachiperi, previously also known as Mashco, originated from the proto-Arahuac linguistic family. They came to the area approximately one thousand years ago, after being displaced from the Ucayali River by other indigenous groups of the Pano ethno-linguistic family. All of these groups are believed to originally come from either Venezuela or northern Peru (Llosa and Nieto 2003: 51–53).

Once established, the territory of the Wachiperi covered a wide geographical area, ranging from the forested Andean hills to the lowland rain forest. As Califano pointed out, the limits of their territory expanded to the top of the Tres Cruces Mountain to the north, the village of Atalaya to the south, the hilltops of the mountains that mark the division with the Urubamba basin to the west, and the headwaters of the Carbon River to the east. Their neighbors were the Toyeri on the north, the Incas and Andean Keros on the south, the Zapiteri on the east, and the Matsiguenka on the west (Califano 1982: 67–69). The Wachiperi mostly lived in the middle and upper parts of the Queros, Blanco, Entoro, Sabaluyoc, Huaysampilla, Tono, and Pillcopata Rivers. The center of the valley was less inhabited by the Wachiperi, because they preferred to build their houses near the hills.

The Wachiperi language is a variation of *Harakmbut Hate*, which means the language of the Harakmbut (Helberg 1987: 1; Lyon 1975). Other Harakmbut groups also spoke variations of Harakmbut Hate. Besides the Wachiperi, the Harakmbut family included the Amarakaeri, Toyeri, Sapiteri, Arasairi, Kareneri, Tuyuneri, and others (Barriales and Torralba 1970: 5; Lyon 1975: 13; Helberg 1996: 16). Today, almost everyone in Queros speaks Spanish in addition to Wachiperi. In their everyday communications, senior members of the community use mostly Wachiperi, but the younger generation of adults uses Spanish on a more frequent basis.

The term *Wachiperi* means "builders of wooden bridges." Scholars have proposed different explanations for the origins of the term Wachiperi, but the most likely scenario is that this word was used by other Harakmbut groups to refer to the Wachiperi. As Califano suggested, the word *huachipa* might have come from the term "huatshipa," which means bridge, alluding to the skill of the Wachiperi to build bridges over streams using wooden materials (1982: 67). The area they inhabited had plenty of streams, which created the need for people to build wooden bridges and cross them on a frequent basis. Regarding spelling, the most common form used in the past was *Huachipaeri*, in addition to other variations like *Wachipaeri*, *Huachipaire*, *Wachipairi*, *Wacipire*, and *Oatipaeri*. The term adopted in this book is *Wachiperi*, which follows the current decision of people from Queros to redefine the spelling of this word in the way they consider more appropriate. This change is in the process of being incorporated into the community statute (Queros 1996), which is a written document that contains a set of agreed regulations to guide the collective behavior of its members.

The Amazonian environment has not favored the preservation of physical evidence of the ancient Wachiperi because most of their material production was made of biodegradable materials. However, one important element that has remained is a giant rock with petroglyphs. In the indigenous language, this rock is known as *Hinkiori*. It is located on the right margin of the Queros River, about halfway between the community of Queros and the town of Pillcopata. Much of Hinkiori is buried in the ground, but the visible part is approximately seven meters wide, six meters deep, and five meters tall. Numerous figures have been carved in the rock. Two carvings that resemble an arrow and its target suggest the possibility that hunting may have been an important activity for the indigenous population in ancient times.

The precise meaning of Hinkiori and the interpretation of its symbols has been for the most part lost in time. However, fragments of this knowledge still exist. As a spiritual leader of the Wachiperi described it, Hinkiori is an entity with deep spiritual meaning. The Wachiperi went there to meditate, to ask for good health and a good life for them and their relatives, to obtain good agricultural production, to find river spots with plenty of fish, and to hunt plenty of animals in the forest, among other activities.

Another important rock with spiritual meaning in the area is Amana, which in ancient times was used by the Wachiperi as an oracle. They believed that when their enemies came to the area they bewitched it, and as a result Amana lost its magical properties and stopped answering to people. Amana is located in the Sabaluyoc sector, within lands currently owned by settlers who came from the Andean region in previous decades. A similar situation happened in the case of Hinkiori, since the area where it is located borders the private property of another settler. Access to Hinkiori from the road requires passing through the lands of this settler, which according to local reports is frustrated by the fact that he does not receive any benefits from these visits and considers visitors mostly as a disturbance to his agricultural crops. In 2006 the Peruvian government started a study (Andrade et al. 2006) to support the legal recognition of Hinkiori as a cultural heritage site, but this study was cut in 2008 due to lack of funding.

According to Moore, Harakmbut groups did not have a hierarchical power structure, but rather a system mainly characterized by "a communalistic and egalitarian form of social organization" (1979: 113). However, this custom did not preclude the existence of leadership abilities based on the personal qualities of individuals. Likewise, Helberg described that in times of conflict the Harakmbut adopted a clearly defined military hierarchy. The maximum chief who led the operations against other groups was called *oantopa*; individuals who had previously participated in a winning battle were called *oairi*, and people who had no conflict experience or had lost a battle were called *oamba* (Helberg 1996: 19). Today, the term *wantopa* is still used to describe the most important member in a group, such as the president of the community, the spiritual entity that serves as chief of forest animal species, and other roles where hierarchies are used.

The Wachiperi used to have alternating periods of violence and peace in their interactions with other groups, including the Incas, whose domain reached the southern borderlands of Wachiperi territory. According to descriptions provided by Garcilaso de la Vega, around the year 1400 the Inca Yupanqui led an expedition of ten thousand people to conquer this region. This expedition faced violent opposition from the indigenous inhabitants, who constantly attacked the outsiders (Califano 1985: 7). These attacks prevented the conquest of their territory and the establishment of Inca settlements in the area. However, peaceful exchanges took place between the Incas and the indigenous population, and agreements were reached to provide the Incas with forest and agricultural products. As Llosa and Nieto described, the indigenous population of the jungle provided the Incas with coca leaves, animals, feathers of birds, ornamental seeds, arrow and spear heads made out of wood, pepper, cotton, peanuts, sweet potatoes, honey, vegetable ink, medicinal plants, fishing poison roots, gold powder, bat pelts, snake oil, and pets such as parrots, macaws, and monkeys. In exchange, the indigenous groups from the jungle received products like dried meat, machetes, and other metal tools (Llosa and Nieto 2003).

Resistance and Conflict

During the colonial period, which in Peru started in 1532, different Spanish expeditions who went to the Kosñipata Valley faced the opposition of local indigenous groups. Califano wrote that many Spaniards arrived in the area searching for the "Paititi," a mythical city hidden in the forest containing golden treasures. The most outstanding expeditions were those of Pedro de Candia in 1538 and Juan Alvarez de Maldonado in 1566. The Spanish explorers faced multiple attacks by the indigenous population, which prevented these expeditions from succeeding (Califano 1985: 7).

In the middle of the sixteenth century, the discovery of mining resources in Potosí, located in current Bolivian territory, stimulated the production of coca leaves. The growing trade of coca leaves made this a profitable enterprise, and many Spaniards took over the coca plantations in the Kosñipata Valley that previously supplied the Incas with this product (Llosa and Nieto 2003: 34). Coca leaves became an important commodity because mineworkers performed their jobs significantly better when they consumed them. Consumption of coca leaves reduced the fatigue, pain, and discomfort associated with difficult working conditions. The coca leaves produced in the Kosñipata Valley were of high quality, which promoted the establishment of more Spanish agricultural plantations in the area.

Plantations grew and declined according to the demands of the regional and international markets and the prices of commodities in different historical moments. One of the most significant difficulties plantation owners experienced was the continuous attacks of the indigenous population. Attempts to incorporate them into the labor force of the plantations were unsuccessful, and indigenous raids on plantations were common during the colonial period.

The Catholic priest Joseph de Velasco y Villagra described the presence of the "mata chuncho," a sentinel position created to protect people living on the plantations from indigenous attacks, who had to stand guard with their weapons ready at all times (Escalante and Valderrama 2000: 37). This fear of indigenous attacks could have been an important factor preventing the establishment of peaceful relations. As Califano described, armed people on the plantations sometimes opened fire on the Wachiperi without giving them time to explain themselves, shooting them on first sight. This reception prevented attempts at peaceful interactions and discouraged the Wachiperi from further efforts to communicate with the plantation dwellers (Califano 1985: 8).

While extractive activities in the Amazon region can be traced to five hundred years of progressive Western exploitation of tropical forests, in the specific case of the Kosñipata Valley, the exploitation of natural resources was for the most part conducted without the participation of the indigenous population. The extractive activities of the plantations in the region (originally owned by the Spanish and afterwards by their descendants) became more intense during the colonial period due to the growing demand for agricultural products. As plantation owner Abel Muñiz described, based on oral accounts of his grandparents, the early plantations mainly grew coca leaves, cacao, and sugar cane for the production of aguardiente, a distilled liquor similar to brandy.

Other major agricultural crops produced in the Kosñipata Valley were coffee, tea, cotton, beans, and rice (Llosa and Nieto 2003: 38–40). At some point there were up to three hundred plantations in the area. However, in the nineteenth century most plantations were abandoned or transferred to new owners. This situation was the result of the country's political independence, as well as the new laws and restrictions relating to the trade of goods from plantations located in the rain forest, which affected the viability of the plantations (Escalante and Valderrama 2000: 132–138).

Plantations in the Jungle

The Republican period in Peru started in 1821, when General José de San Martin declared the independence of Peru from Spain. The control of the country was then assumed by an oligarchy composed of the descendants of Spaniards born in Peru (*criollos*), who retained control of most of the land and acquired greater political power. Other foreigners who came to the Kosñipata Valley also became plantation owners, including the Spaniard Bernardino Perdiz, the Swede Sven Erikson, the Japanese Antonio Ibaki and Vicente Enoki, among others (Escalante and Valderrama 2000: 132–138).

During this period, plantations in the Kosñipata Valley continued harvesting forest products from the region according to the demands of the regional and international markets. As Llosa and Nieto wrote, these products included medicinal plants like cinchona, which was used by the indigenous population to cure malaria; latex from rubber trees to supply the industrial demands of industrialized countries; timber harvesting, particularly cedar and mahogany, as well as Brazil nuts and tropical fish (Llosa and Nieto 2003: 39–43).

In the Republican period, the Wachiperi and other indigenous groups in the area still remained away from the plantations. The failure of early missionaries to convert the Wachiperi to the Christian faith was an important factor that contributed to maintaining their independence. The fact that the indigenous population of the Kosñipata Valley remained away from the plantations forced plantation owners to import workers. As Escalante and Valderrama reported, this was the case of Bernardino Perdiz, who brought seventy indigenous families from the Bora group from the Putumayo River in Colombia. After working for some time, they decided to leave the plantation and return to their homeland. These workers were then replaced by prisoners. According to the laws of that time, prisoners could be sent to work on the plantations of the jungle, reducing their terms while also being paid for their labor. However, there was a system of corruption that favored a series of human rights violations. Many people from the Andean region were victims of false charges like robbery so that plantations could obtain the labor force they needed. Moreover, after prisoners had completed their term and were paid for their services, they were ambushed and killed under orders of plantation owners, who recovered the money previously paid to the workers (Escalante and Valderrama 2000: 134–138). This situation promoted fear among potential recruits in the Andean region, who were afraid of being enslaved or killed in the jungle, affecting the availability of plantation workers.

The scarcity of workers encouraged missionaries and plantation owners to make efforts to befriend the indigenous population and incorporate them into their labor force, but these efforts were for the most part unsuccessful. As Fernández described, in 1902 the Catholic priest Zubieta made a visit to a colonial plantation in the Kosñipata Valley. Since the owner of the plantation was at the time on good trading terms with the Wachiperi, he contacted them to come and meet the missionary. The Wachiperi sent a delegation of eight people, meeting the priest and receiving abundant gifts from him (Fernández 1952: 59). This encounter indicates that around that time there were some peaceful interactions and occasional visits between the Wachiperi and the plantation owners. However, the Wachiperi still preferred to stay away from the plantations, sending only a few individuals to trade products. These individuals were usually men. The Wachiperi were also wary of the gifts received, since they were afraid of catching diseases. They believed that illnesses could be embedded in the food they received. As a member of Queros recalled, "They were afraid of bread because they believed it could have the flu embedded, so they had to rub it several times for the disease to go away before eating it."

The Wachiperi also lived far away from the plantations. Wachiperi elders recall that until the 1950s they did not live in villages but scattered in the Kosñipata Valley. Houses were located a few kilometers from each other and were generally associated with the stream or river closest to them. Lyon wrote that Wachiperi houses were rectangular with rounded ends and doorways at each end, measured about thirty meters long by twelve meters wide, and contained multiple nuclear families (1967: 17). The inside area had no physical divisions, but each family had their own bed, which defined their own spatial location in the house. According to a person from Queros, "Each family had their own little hearth and bed platform."

In terms of dressing style, when it was warm the Wachiperi wore crowns and collars, which constituted their formal attire. They also tied strings on their arms and legs, which served as pockets. Sometimes they also painted their bodies. Some men wore feathers on their faces, resembling the whiskers of a jaguar. In colder weather, their clothing consisted of beige robes (*hotto*) made out of the bark of a tree (*hiri*), which was beaten and stretched until it became a soft layer (see Figure 2). These robes usually included drawings of forest animals and symbols found on Hinkiori, but they have also added new external elements. Today, the Wachiperi normally wear Western clothes purchased in the market of Pillcopata.

Figure 2. Traditional clothing of the Wachiperi

The pattern of a cyclical perception of peace and conflict, as evidenced in the case of their interactions with the plantation dwellers, was influenced by their ancestral myths and traditions. Conflicts with other indigenous groups were common, including those from the same linguistic family who spoke variations of Harakmbut Hate. In peaceful times, frequent exchanges took place between members of these groups. As reported by Califano, some Zapiteri came to live with the Wachiperi, especially individuals who were in self-exile due to disagreements with members of their group, finding new partners among the Wachiperi (1982: 69).

Outsiders were generally addressed by the Wachiperi with the term *amiko*. Califano reported that this term was initially used to refer to the Incas, and later expanded to the Spaniards and other foreigners who owned the colonial plantations in the area (1985: 8). More recently, the term amiko was used to address former Andean settlers currently living in the Kosñipata Valley. All of these groups are referred to as outsiders here, with the understanding that there are different degrees of externality and that the division between insiders and outsiders is sometimes flexible and permeable. Conversely, indigenous groups in the region speaking Harakmbut Hate were not considered amiko but addressed as Harakmbut in times of peace or *baeri* in times of war.

Most conflicts with other Harakmbut groups happened along the Sabaluyoc River, which was originally called *Wayombi* in the Wachiperi language. The main reason for the conflicts was most likely competition for natural resources, since the Sabaluyoc River was rich in fish. As an elderly person from Queros recalled, "They wanted to take over that area because it was a good place and there were lots of fish." A common fishing technique used by the local indigenous groups was to spread barbasco *(Lonchocarpus sp.)* in the water, a toxic substance that made fish drowsy. With this technique, once a group fished in a section of the river, it was difficult for others to obtain any significant amount of fish nearby, forcing them to go somewhere else or wait until the fish population replenished. Under this modality, only the group who arrived first benefited with an abundant harvest. Accordingly, conflicts often started when different groups ran into each other when they went fishing, and each of them tried to chase the other away. Since they did not have agreed territorial boundaries, these groups felt entitled to the resources of the area and none of them wanted to withdraw. Fruitless discussions led to clashes, which often led them to finally agree on something, the time for a battle. When that happened, most women and children were sent away from the fighting zone. In some cases, however, men also started to shoot arrows at each other on the spot, which produced many dead and wounded. This was considered a serious offense because these injuries were not the result of agreed battles. In response, the other groups in the area, such as the Toyeri and Zapiteri, organized raiding parties at night, attacking the houses of the Wachiperi. The main purposes of these raids were to avenge their relatives and friends, to kidnap women who were later made wives of their captors, and an attempt to exert supremacy over access to the natural resources in areas bordering their territories.

These types of conflicts happened on a recurrent basis, but at some point they escalated into a large-scale conflict with the Toyeri. This happened around 1940. The Wachiperi recall that there was a big battle at the intersection of the Istare and Sabaluyoc Rivers. A huge number of warriors on both sides died at that time, so many that the remains of the dead could be found in the river for months. As a result, the name of the Sabaluyoc River was changed from Wayombi to Waywe, which means "river of the bones" in Wachiperi. As a woman from Queros described it, "Dead people decomposed there and later there were lots of bones, so when the river grew it spread all those bones along the riverbanks."

This crucial battle was won by the Wachiperi, but at a very high cost of their own population and social balance. Defeated, the Toyeri finally retreated from the area. This devastating episode contributed to the later disappearance of the Toyeri as an indigenous group. Today it is believed that there are only a few surviving Toyeri individuals, assimilated into other indigenous communities of the region.

The familiarity of the Wachiperi with conflict situations, along with the fact that early religious conversion was unsuccessful among them, were important factors in preventing their labor exploitation on the plantations. This situation placed the Wachiperi in a privileged position, since it allowed them to maintain their independence in better terms than other indigenous groups in the Amazon region. Maintaining their customary lifestyle contributed to keeping alive their knowledge about the ways of interacting with forest animals, and spiritual entities, in ways that were not significantly affected by Western influences, including hunting, which in the ancestral Wachiperi perception was regarded as an important means of socialization. As such, their culture encouraged the continuity of practices like hunting.

The resistance of the Wachiperi to external attempts to dominate them until the twentieth century was a historical phenomenon uncommon in the region. In other parts of the Amazon region, indigenous peoples had for the most part been subject to religious influence and Spanish domination since the beginning of the Spanish occupation in the sixteenth century. As Lathrap described, most Amazonian societies "were very early disrupted by the effects of slave raiding, missionization, and diseases introduced by the Europeans" (1973: 83). Rejecting the invitations to be incorporated into the labor force of the plantations and the religious conversion attempts of early missionaries helped the Wachiperi maintain their independence, favoring the continuity of their customary way of life without preventing them from accessing external goods.

Gifts from the Newcomers

The independent lifestyle of the Wachiperi changed around the middle of the twentieth century when their degree of interaction with outsiders significantly increased. During one of the product exchanges with people on the plantations, some Wachiperi acquired smallpox, which spread quickly among them. The introduction of this external disease reduced their population dramatically, making it increasingly difficult to sustain their traditional lifestyle. As a member from Queros described it, "We could not go on anymore."

The introduction of contagious diseases was devastating for the Wachiperi. As an elderly person from Queros recalled, "Lots of people died, including women and children, the ones who survived were only a minimal part." The deaths created emotional distress and deep social disruptions. The Wachiperi quietly buried their dead inside their homes, since there were not enough people to conduct preparations for ceremonial burials with singing and drinking, which was the customary practice. During these times of profound sorrow, they mostly cried. Some people also abandoned their houses and went to live with relatives, creating challenges in terms of living arrangements and sustenance. They still managed to conduct their subsistence activities but at a reduced rate compared to the levels displayed before their demographic decline.

The transmission of external diseases was a key factor in changing the lives of the Wachiperi. External diseases were particularly harmful for the Wachiperi because their immune systems had not been previously exposed to them. The general characteristics of the patterns of disease and mortality among the Wachiperi before they established permanent relationships with members of Western society included accidents and traumatic deaths, parasitic infections, snakebites, chronic illnesses, and vector-transmitted diseases like malaria and yellow fewer.

In the case of hunting, it is also likely that some illnesses might have been transmitted from forest animals to the Wachiperi, especially when the people butchering the animals had open wounds, putting them in close contact with the animal's blood. Other illnesses likely to have been transmitted from animals were skin diseases, fungus, ticks, lice, and different types of parasites. However, after centuries of being exposed to these health risks, indigenous peoples tend to develop some level of biological resistance and cultural strategies to prevent or cope with these illnesses, increasing their levels of resilience.

Newly introduced contagious diseases were different and as a result created dramatic impacts in the indigenous populations' survival as a group. As Pinasco described, approximately 65% of the Wachiperi died as a result of the outbreak of smallpox brought by outsiders (2002: 13). In the words of an elderly woman from the community of Queros, "When this new disease appeared many people departed, it was sad, here and there people murmured 'I am going to die,' and as time passed they died." The Wachiperi reported that the massive deaths and their associated impacts on their way of life forced them to look for alternatives, and they decided to accept the invitation of Baptist missionaries to move with them to a mission located nearby, between the Queros and Entoro Rivers. As a man from Queros recalled, "When the missionaries came they called us, so we finally decided to go and stay in the mission." The missionaries also provided health support for the survivors, in some cases sending some of them to the city of Cusco to receive medical care.

The rapid decrease of the Wachiperi population profoundly changed their traditional way of life, disrupting their social interactions, their relationship with the environment, and their subsistence practices, including a temporary reduction in their hunting practices. Many surviving hunters whose wives and other relatives died had to carry out tasks near their houses more frequently, such as gathering firewood or harvesting agricultural products, reducing their available time to go hunting. In a similar way, hunters that were accustomed to going to the forest in small groups were often saddened by the deaths of fellow hunting party members. Accordingly, the emotional and practical implications of losing a friend or relative affected their everyday practices, creating deep social disruptions that temporarily decreased the frequency of hunting.

The concentration of the Wachiperi in a single settlement and their increased interactions with missionaries and other visitors to the mission also placed them at high risk for new diseases. As Pinasco described, the arrival of greater numbers of settlers to the area also helped spread other illnesses among them, especially new strains of the flu, cough, and tuberculosis (2002: 13). Another significant disease transmitted to the Wachiperi was chicken pox, which reappeared every five years or so. Tuberculosis has also been recurrent in the last few decades, especially among the elderly. Illnesses that so far have not been diagnosed among the Wachiperi include heart diseases, mental health problems, diabetes, and sexually transmitted diseases. A list of the most common diseases among the Wachiperi is presented in Table 1.

Until the middle of the twentieth century, the Wachiperi dealt with illnesses using a combination of medicinal plants and healing chants. They had healing songs called *eshuwa*. The healers who cured others of both physical and spiritual illnesses were called *wamanokaeri*. They also cleansed people of the ill-intended spells of malefic sorcerers, which were called *wachindintewamanca*. Healing was an activity that inspired high respect among other members of the group. Most wamanokaeri were male, but there were some cases of women healers as well. This was not a full-time occupation, since healers' help was mainly required when there were complicated health problems. Most adult Wachiperi had some knowledge of healing songs and medicinal plants to treat common ailments like snakebites, diarrhea, stomachaches, body aches, fever, vomiting, headaches, wounds, and others.

Table 1. Common Illnesses among the Wachiperi

Traditional Illnesses	Spanish Name	Wachiperi Name
Body ache	Dolor de cuerpo	Embachiri
Stomachache	Dolor de estómago	Eminchiri
Earache	Dolor de oído	Pehechiri
Diarrhea	Diarrea	Wamieka
Toothache	Dolor de dientes	Einchiri
Headache	Dolor de cabeza	Ecuchiri
Fever	Fiebre	Endinpac
Wounds	Heridas	Embasete
Vomit	Vómito	Ehoc
Kidney disease	Inflamación de riñones	Watapikind dinehe
Stye	Ursuelo	Ecpohan
Fungus (feet)	Hongos	Echihid
Snakebites	Picadura de serpiente	Embooc
Malaria	Malaria	Endinpac
Yellow fever	Fiebre amarilla	Ehirinna
Animal-induced illness	Cutipado	Dingaehe
Panic illness	Susto	Emepuc
Nightmares	Pesadilla	Embayoroga

New Illnesses	Spanish Name	Wachiperi Name
Smallpox	Viruela	----
Chicken pox	Varicela	----
Flu	Gripe	Soron
Cough	Tos	Eyuhu
Tuberculosis	Tuberculosis	Wanopoyan dinehe
Parasites	Parásitos	Supi
Cancer	Cáncer	----
Gastritis	Gastritis	----
Gastric ulcer	Ulcera gástrica	----

Note: Cells containing "----" indicate that this term does not exist in Wachiperi.

Nowadays, the most common way of treating their illnesses is with a combination of medicinal plants and Western medicine. Their first choice is generally the use of medicinal plants, which people from Queros use on a regular basis. Considerable knowledge about the use of medicinal plants is still present and is passed on to younger generations, even if it is only a small fraction of the knowledge they had in previous decades. Their second choice is typically buying self-prescribed drugs in Pillcopata, either at the pharmacy in the health center or from corner stores that sell medication such as antibiotics without prescription. Their third choice is generally to see a doctor in the health center of Pillcopata, a local branch of the Peruvian Ministry of Health. They use this health center when there is a more serious problem or the patient's health has already deteriorated to a considerable extent.

Currently, people from Queros are covered by a basic government-financed insurance plan, so costs are not much of an issue now, but the quality of health services is reported to be poor. Many people from Queros try to avoid going to the health center because they feel that its staff treats indigenous peoples as second-class patients, usually taking care of urban dwellers first. It is possible that these delays in attention have to do with the additional time required to process the insurance paperwork of indigenous patients, but they also suggest a situation of ethnic and social discrimination against indigenous and rural populations. Many members of Queros also believe that the nurses at the health center are under-qualified to perform their duties, since there is an alleged history of patient deaths as a result of mistakes like administering the wrong prescriptions or excessive doses of medication. Consequently, most people from Queros prefer to buy medicine in the pharmacy and self-medicate as a preferred alternative to seeking attention at the health center of Pillcopata, except in cases of serious complications.

The growing interaction between the Wachiperi and outsiders introduced new socioeconomic and cultural elements that produced changes in the Wachiperi way of life. These changes included the adoption of new crops, which expanded their choices of agricultural activities. Also, when firearms were introduced they promoted hunting activities and contributed to a temporary intensification in Wachiperi hunting practices. As a person from Queros recalled, "We were given shotguns in exchange for work when the missionaries arrived." The adoption of shotguns made them progressively abandon the use of the bow and arrow, and after the Wachiperi moved out of the Baptist mission they only used arrows for fishing, not for hunting anymore. The greater availability of metal tools, like machetes, also promoted the intensification of their agricultural production.

An important harvesting activity that affected the availability of wildlife in the region was fur trade. Between 1950 and 1970 in particular, many hunters from other regions came to the Kosñipata Valley in search of pelts. Animals were killed and their pelts tanned for export, providing the raw materials to make clothing, shoes, purses, and belts. As a result of commercial hunting, the population of some of these animals was severely affected. Hunting for collections of tropical animals also took place in different areas across the world (Llosa and Nieto 2003: 43). Pelt trade is still allowed by Peruvian law today and is widely practiced in the Amazon region. There are annual limits for the trade of pelts, but traders often exceed these limits (Lleellish et al. 2007). However, the Wachiperi were not involved in any fur trade activity. When they worked in the plantations, which was done for short periods and only until they could exchange their labor for metal tools or clothing, they did not trade animal pelts.

Struggles for land were also significant in this area, especially during the second half of the twentieth century. These struggles were directly associated with the growing presence of settlers and the improved means of transportation. The city of Cusco and the plantations in the Kosñipata Valley were connected by narrow trails of difficult access until plantation owners made gradual improvements to these trails, encouraged by the need to sell their products. As Abel Muñiz explained, in 1905, plantation owners improved the access trail to allow horses loaded with their products to reach the town of Paucartambo and the city of Cusco. In 1930, the trail from Paucartambo to Pillcopata was expanded into a dirt road whose farthest point was San Pedro on the upper side of the Kosñipata Valley. A dirt path reached Pillcopata approximately in 1955, and in 1960, further improvements allowed carts pulled by oxen to carry local products. In the 1970s, Peru's national government converted this trail into a dirt road, which allowed trucks to reach the area and transport heavier loads.

The arrival of settlers to the region on a larger scale started in the 1970s. Improvements in road conditions encouraged the movement of people from other parts of the country, especially from the Andean region. They expanded the towns of Patria and Pillcopata and opened new areas for agricultural production in their surroundings. As Contreras described, this movement of people was also encouraged by policies of the Peruvian government supporting the colonization of the jungle (2007: 8). Around that time, the official discourse was that the jungle was an empty space that needed courageous people to move there and exploit its abundant natural resources (Santos 1985). This migratory movement generated a competition for land in the region, and in the lapse of a few years, the Wachiperi saw themselves surrounded by newcomers.

The case of the population that settled in the sector of Tupac Amaru, located on the northwestern side of Queros, is an example of this colonization process. It also illustrates the transition from plantations to independent farms, characteristic of what happened in the region. Since the 1930s, people from the Andean regions of Sicuani and Paucartambo were hired to work on the plantations of the Kosñipata Valley and to transport the goods they produced. Some important plantations were Santa Ines, San Julian, Atalaya, Ubaldina, San Victor, Carazas, Laura, and Yabar. In 1969, agrarian reform allowed plantation workers to take ownership of the land where they had been working. Taking advantage of these changes, many workers brought their friends and relatives from the Andean region to the Kosñipata Valley. The newcomers pretended to be former plantation workers so they could benefit from the changing laws regarding land ownership. At the beginning of the transition, there was a struggle between the workers and the former plantation owners. In some cases there were conflicts and in others they held peaceful negotiations. In the end, the workers prevailed in their claims over the ownership of the land, which was later distributed as individual pieces of property. They formed an association of owners called Tupac Amaru and later started functioning as a settlers' rural community.

While these processes happened, the Wachiperi stayed in the Baptist mission until approximately 1970, when disagreements arose between the Wachiperi and the missionaries. As elder members of Queros recalled, the missionaries made it mandatory for young people to attend preaching sessions for two hours each day. Adults were expected to listen to their preaching at night and during the weekends, creating some level of discomfort. At some point, the missionaries also forbade the Wachiperi to continue drinking *masato*, a culturally significant alcoholic beverage that was an important part of their social interactions and conflict resolution, as described by Lyon (1967: 2). These regulations created an uncomfortable situation among the Wachiperi.

The larger disagreement, however, involved cattle. As reported by people from Queros, the Baptist missionary in charge of the Queros mission asked them to bring cattle from the town of Boca Manu, which took them about two weeks of hard labor. The initial agreement was that the cattle were intended for the Wachiperi, but after the cattle were brought in, they were never delivered as promised. The Wachiperi reported that this missionary used the cattle for his own benefit, making people work for him in exchange for tools and shotguns. The cattle also started to ruin the crops and houses of the Wachiperi, and the missionary was unwilling to take corrective measures to fix the problem, making the Wachiperi feel that cattle raising had become the focus of the missionary in charge. Instead of addressing the problems created by the cattle, this missionary made it clear that the Wachiperi were only guests in the mission and could leave it at any time. The Wachiperi were offended by this statement and the aggressive tone employed by the missionary, so they decided to abandon the mission. As a member of the community of Queros stated, "The missionary changed; he lost interest in delivering the word of God and cared mostly about business."

After leaving the mission, the Wachiperi split and went to different places, especially to areas near the Sabaluyoc and Entoro Rivers, as well as the community of Huacaria. Some people also went to a Catholic mission in the community of Shintuya. Thus the Wachiperi remained dispersed until a young member of the group named Alejandro Jahuanchi came back to the area after finishing his training as a teacher and undertook the task of finding a place for the Wachiperi to live together again. As Contreras described, from 1970 to 1973, Jahuanchi led efforts to obtain public lands for the Wachiperi (2007: 9). His efforts were favored by the agrarian reform that was implemented in the country during that period. In 1974, the Peruvian government granted the Wachiperi an area of 2,924 hectares (11.3 square miles), recognizing a space for them in the area where they currently lived. At that time, the Wachiperi regrouped and formed a village, which they named Queros, because the land allocated was next to the Queros River. Queros was recognized as a Native Community[4] on October 4, 1974, via the resolution 140-AE-ORAMS-VII-74. The anniversary of the community is celebrated every year on this day. It is the biggest annual event, which involves conducting hunting parties to obtain plenty of meat for the festivities.

In the lapse of two decades, the Wachiperi had to recover from a situation of great instability generated by both their massive population decline and the changes in their

---

[4] In this case, the term "Native Community" refers to a legal category in the Peruvian legislation introduced in the 1970s (Laws 20653 and 22175). To gain access to lands in areas inhabited by their ancestors, indigenous groups had to become a Native Community and fulfill a number of official requirements.

settlement patterns. After a short period of displacement and dispersion, their regrouping process created the need to adapt to a new set of social dynamics and environmental practices. They also had to adopt a new governance system, following the national law regarding the organization of Native Communities. The Peruvian law required them to elect a council constituted by a president, a secretary, a treasurer, a controller, and a representative. The Wachiperi had to keep written records of the decisions adopted in their community assemblies and develop a statute with their internal regulations, among other requirements. This externally imposed governance structure, necessary to gain official recognition as a juridical entity and obtain access to the land, created a new organizational system, with implications for the Wachiperi's social interactions, including their relationship with the environment and the use of natural resources.

The greater migratory movement of Andean settlers to the area also happened around this time, while the Wachiperi were still adapting to their new way of life as a result of their recent conversion into a Native Community. The increasing arrival of newcomers created the need for the Wachiperi to ensure their territorial rights. This process started in 1974 with their formal recognition as a Native Community by the Peruvian government and concluded in 1990, when they acquired the legal title of their territory. This milestone concluded their struggle for the acquisition of lands, allowing them to plan their future with greater confidence.

The acquisition of community lands, together with the adoption of a new governance system within the Peruvian legislation, provided a space for the Wachiperi to redefine their community life. This recognition allowed them to find a new point of equilibrium, based on the assumption that disturbances "can flip a system from one equilibrium state to another" (Berkes and Folke 1998: 12). This new social and geographical space provided the conditions for the Wachiperi to reinforce their recovery process after the deep social disruptions they had experienced since the middle of the twentieth century. They particularly refer to the massive deaths among them and the impact of the changes in their settlement patterns. Likewise, access to community lands opened the possibility for them to have greater flexibility in the implementation of their subsistence activities and selection of livelihoods in general, within the context of their growing interactions with settlers and their progressive engagement in market activities.

After the recognition of their territory, most Wachiperi families came to live in Queros, but not all of them. Some families had already settled in the community of Huacaria, which consisted of a combination of Matsiguenka, Wachiperi, and Andean settlers. A few Wachiperi families also went to live in the community of Shintuya, one of the farthest points in the region that cargo trucks can reach, about four hours away from Pillcopata. Shintuya is a large indigenous community, mainly populated by members of the Amarakaeri indigenous group, but also by Catholic missionaries, traders, and employees of public institutions like a hospital and school. Another Wachiperi family moved to the community of Diamante, which is located even farther away than Shintuya, where the majority of the population is Yine. Some Wachiperi also settled in the town of Pillcopata but remained active members of Queros. Other community members went to live in the city of Cusco.

While many people went away, others came in. In the past three decades, some individuals from the Andean region have been incorporated as members of Queros, mostly by marrying people from this community. At present, Queros is the only indigenous community consisting mainly of a Wachiperi population, even though most Wachiperi individuals who now live in other places still maintain some type of connection with their friends and relatives in Queros.

These residence patterns indicate that their community has not been an isolated one, but rather has been deeply affected by their relationship with settlers. The community also functioned mainly as a network of people that transcended the bounded space of their community territory. This situation is especially relevant in the case of the Wachiperi who live in

Pillcopata but are still considered full members of the community of Queros. The importance of their collective network is also reflected in their feeling of inclusion toward the Wachiperi that live in other communities and the assimilation of non-indigenous people as members of Queros.

Historical Specificity

This section summarizes the historical sequence of events influencing the intensity of the hunting practices among the Wachiperi. As in many other parts of the world, the influence of the global economy affected the local socioeconomic processes of this region in significant ways. The main economic activities in the Kosñipata Valley were historically based on agricultural production and the harvesting of forest resources by plantations. Plantations flourished and declined according to the demands of the regional and international markets, the prices that commodities acquired in different historical moments, and the government policies affecting regional trade. Colonialism was an important factor that favored the presence of agricultural plantations in the area, as well as the initial flow of settlers that followed, based on the demand for workers created by the plantations. However, commercial harvesting in the Kosñipata Valley took place without the presence of the local indigenous population, which for the most part refused to work on the plantations. As a result, plantation owners had to bring workers from other regions, which increased the number of outsiders in the area but also decreased the pressure to incorporate the indigenous population into their labor force. This allowed the Wachiperi to maintain their traditional worldviews and practices of subsistence, such as hunting and agriculture.

Before the establishment of closer relationships with Western society, conflict with outsiders constituted the most common state of affairs, which lasted until the middle of the twentieth century. This lack of proximity allowed the Wachiperi to maintain the spiritual beliefs associated with their traditional practices of subsistence and the reproduction of their ancestral culture and knowledge relatively independently of the forced imposition of Westerners. This cultural independence placed the Wachiperi in a different position than most Amazonian groups in Peru, which in many cases were culturally assimilated, enslaved, dominated, or forced to live with missionaries and work for the colonizers since the beginning of the Spanish occupation in the sixteenth century.

After Peru's independence from Spain, the conflicts between the Wachiperi and the plantations decreased, allowing the establishment of more frequent exchanges. Greater interactions with outsiders near the middle of the twentieth century favored the transmission of external diseases, which killed a large number of Wachiperi. These deaths disrupted their way of life in dramatic ways, affecting their social interactions and their relationship with the environment, including a temporary reduction in their levels of hunting due to practical and emotional reasons. They resettled into a Baptist mission, replacing their previously scattered houses for a village setting. Their concentration in a single settlement, together with the introduction of shotguns, produced a temporary scarcity of forest animals in the area within a few years. This situation created a need for the Wachiperi to explore alternative means of subsistence.

In the following years, settlers started a process of habitat degradation leading to game scarcity. Even if the Wachiperi were able to maintain the sustainable use of their natural resources, the growing presence of settlers in the surrounding areas became a source of disturbance. Within a few years, the newcomers opened new areas for agricultural production in a continuous way, chasing forest animals away. Accordingly, the frequency of hunting by the Wachiperi decreased, since trips to the forest in search of game became increasingly uncertain, reducing their efficiency levels and increasing their opportunity costs. Thus they soon directed their time and effort toward more reliable activities of production, such as fishing and agriculture. Fishing in particular intensified in the following years to an extent that even endangered the fish population.

In sum, the level of hunting intensity among the Wachiperi experienced a temporary reduction around the middle of the twentieth century. However, this decrease in hunting intensity was not a constant trend, since their hunting practices also seem to have experienced temporary periods of intensification in the following decades, especially after the introduction of new hunting technologies. These historical and socioeconomic processes contributed to shaping the early environmental behavior of the Wachiperi. As Igoe stated, "Colonial histories have shaped indigenous livelihoods and social organization in ways that have fundamental implications for local conservation" (2004: 177). History not only placed the Wachiperi within the processes shaped by colonialism, but also set them apart from the experience of most indigenous groups in the Amazon region, since the Wachiperi were able to retain a greater degree of cultural independence until recently.

The influence of specific historical processes, however, does not preclude the existence of cross-cultural factors, which were also influential in hunting intensity. They refer to factors such as cultural changes, market demands, technological acquisitions, and the diversification of livelihoods. Changes in social roles also had direct implications on indigenous environmental behavior, especially when they affected areas like gender and labor. The relevance of changes in gender roles will be addressed in the next chapter, which focuses on the subsistence activities of the Wachiperi from a perspective based on their gendered division of labor. The next chapter also describes Wachiperi hunting practices in more detail.

Chapter II

Hunting and the Division of Labor

When I started interviewing the Wachiperi, I was told by several people that hunting was an activity conducted only by men. Later in my research I talked to an elderly woman in the community who used to hunt, before the years blurred her vision and took much of her strength away. Listening to her made me reflect about the role of women in hunting, which seemed to offer promising ethnographic insights, despite repeated reports by other members of the community dismissing the relevance of women in this activity. I pursued this line of exploration, adding a gendered perspective to my analysis. This pursuit proved to be rewarding, since it led me to perceive the importance of gender roles and expanded the scope of my analysis in a more inclusive way.

This chapter addresses the relevance of gender roles in the hunting practices of the Wachiperi through the analysis of their gendered division of labor. The notion of social roles is understood here in a flexible way as the position of people in society, which generally defines "a social identity that carries with it a certain range (however diffusely specified) of prerogatives and obligations" (Giddens 1984: 84). Gender roles are also approached from a livelihoods perspective, which considers the combined contribution of both men and women to the productive activities of the group as a whole. Special attention is paid to the role of women in hunting activities, since the role of women in hunting has for the most part been excluded from ethnographic accounts (Stange 1997: 2; Slocum

2004: 478; Estioko-Griffin 1993: 225). In addition to hunting, the chapter also describes other subsistence practices like agriculture, fishing, gathering, trading, and household chores, considering the gendered division of labor within each of them.

A summarized list representing the traditional and contemporary subsistence activities of the Wachiperi by gender is included in Table 2. However, it is important to recognize that this table is only a simplified representation of Wachiperi labor roles and is useful only as a starting point of analysis, because in practice the activities of men and women have diffuse borders and fluid interconnections. A table format also prevents a clear appreciation of the collaboration between women and men, as well as the complementary activities that enable them to fulfill their gendered tasks. Examples include the role of women distributing and cooking the meat obtained from hunting, which enabled the group in general to benefit from the product of the hunt, or situations when women joined their husbands on hunting trips and in logging camps, carrying out activities that usually went unnoticed.

This chapter also explores the changes in Wachiperi social roles during the last few decades, focusing on their implications for hunting and other subsistence activities.[5] As discussed later in this chapter, the roles of Wachiperi men and women have experienced significant changes since the middle of the twentieth century, and these changes have increasingly influenced their everyday practices. The chapter ends with a discussion about the influence of gender on hunting, reflecting on the implications of changing gender relations on the environmental behavior of the Wachiperi and illustrating how hunting has been shaped by multiple factors at different levels.

---

[5] In this book, hunting is understood as the regular search for non-domesticated animals in the forest or on the riverbanks with the specific purpose of procuring the meat of these animals. Killing these animals without a clear intentionality or without displaying a recurrent pattern is not considered hunting per se. This definition is based on criteria shared by most Wachiperi men and women.

Hunting Practices

Before the establishment of permanent relationships with members of Western society, hunting was an important subsistence activity of the Wachiperi and other indigenous peoples in the area. As Lathrap pointed out, indigenous groups in the Amazon region who inhabited areas distant from the large rivers "relied heavily on the hunting of terrestrial and arboreal game for their subsistence" (1973: 84). Clay also argued that "indigenous peoples throughout Latin American tropical rain forests depended upon hunted animals for large portions of their food calories and, in many cases, for most of their protein" (1988: 11).

Among the Wachiperi, the meat of forest animals was important in their diet. According to Lyon, "A Wachipaeri did not really consider that he had eaten if there was no meat in the meal, and considerable reluctance was shown to inviting someone to eat if there was no meat available" (1967: 12). While the importance of hunting among the Wachiperi has decreased in the last decades, hunting is still significant among them. Today, the main animals hunted by the Wachiperi are small and medium-sized terrestrial mammals and birds. Three of the main criteria for animal preference are taste, body mass, and tenderness of the meat.

The most common terrestrial animals hunted include paca, armadillo, peccaries, tapir, deer, brown agouti, and capybara. Monkeys are the least preferred edible animals to hunt, mainly due to their human resemblance, small size, and hard meat. The birds that are hunted most often include common piping guan, spix's guan, white-throated tinamou, razor-billed curassow, and macaws. Amazonian birds are usually tasty and easy to chew once they are cooked, but they are generally not big enough for people to share with other family members. Table 3 provides a detailed list of the animals they normally hunt.

Table 2. Gendered Division of Labor among the Wachiperi

Traditional Activities	Men	Women
Agriculture	X	XXX
Hunting	XXX	X
Gathering	X	XXX
Fishing	XXX	XXX
Warfare	XXX	X
Trading	X	---
Cooking	---	XXX
Gathering firewood	X	X
Caring for children	---	XXX
Raising animals	---	X
Using medicinal plants	XX	XX
Building houses	XX	X
Making bows and arrows	XXX	X
Making clothes	X	XXX
Making baskets	---	XX
Making bags	---	XX

Contemporary Activities	Men	Women
Agriculture	XXX	XXX
Hunting	X	---
Gathering	X	X
Fishing	X	X
Trading	XX	X
Cooking	---	XXX
Gathering firewood	X	X
Building houses	XX	X
Caring for children	---	XXX
Raising animals	---	XX
Using medicinal plants	X	X
Making handicrafts	X	XX
Ranger	XXX	---
Teacher	X	---
Transportation	X	---

Note: A higher number of "X" reflects greater participation

Before increased contact between the Wachiperi and outsiders around the middle of the twentieth century, the main purpose of hunting among the Wachiperi was for nutritional reasons. However, in the last three decades, hunting expeditions have also been organized to celebrate special occasions like the anniversary of the community creation in October and *carnaval*, a festivity held each year in February.[6] On these occasions, the community gathers and appoints a hunting party whose main task is to go to the forest and bring back abundant meat for the festivities. Pictures of some of the animals commonly hunted by people of Queros are also shown (see Figures 3, 4, and 5).

Smaller hunting trips are also organized independently by individuals for the celebration of birthdays, the inauguration of a new infrastructure project, and the reception of groups of visitors, among other special occasions. On ordinary hunting trips not associated with community events, people often bring their friends along for company, making the hunting trips more enjoyable. The most common situation is when two people go hunting together.

Hunting in Queros is also a form of pest control, a strategy adopted by people to protect their crops, especially cassava and corn. When forest animals come near the agricultural fields in search of edible roots or crops, they often leave visible tracks. When this happens, men in the community set traps or wait for them for the next few days, because it is likely that the animal will return looking for food again. Traps (*maspote*) are also used by men to capture birds, especially doves. The animal species most frequently found near the fields are paca, collared peccary, brown agouti, and small birds.

---

[6] This festivity is related to other carnival celebrations worldwide. It was established after the creation of Queros in 1974 and adopted as part of a combination of external traditions with elements of their ancestral culture, such as the organization of hunting parties associated with carnival celebrations.

Table 3. Animals Hunted by the Wachiperi

Mammals	Local Spanish	Wachiperi	Scientific
Armadillo	Quirquincho	Vasiwekpo	*Dasypus novemcinctus*
Brown agouti	Sihuayro	Huy	*Dasyprocta variegata*
Capuchin monkey	Mono martín	Hoo	*Cebus apella*
Capybara	Ronsoco	Asign	*Hydrochaeris hydrochaeris*
Coati	Achuni	Capihi	*Nasua nasua*
Collared peccary	Sajino	Mukas	*Tayassu tajacu*
Giant armadillo	Quintalero	Acoro	*Priodontes maximus*
Paca	Picuro	Cayare	*Agouti paca*
Red brocket deer	Venado	Vahi	*Mazama americana*
Red howler monkey	Cotomono	Sowe	*Alouatta seniculus*
Spider monkey	Maquisapa	Machira	*Ateles belzebuth*
Tapir	Sachavaca	Washewi	*Tapirus terrestris*
White-lipped peccary	Huangana	Yari	*Tayassu pecari*
Woolly monkey	Mono choro	Toyore	*Lagothrix lagothricha*

Birds	Local Spanish	Wachiperi	Scientific
Blue and gold macaw	Boliviano	Yonca	*Ara ararauna*
Common piping guan	Pava de monte	Kisi	*Aburria pipile*
Mealy Amazon	Aurora	Saro	*Amazona farinose*
Pale-winged trumpeter	Trompetero	Tsuru	*Psophia leucoptera*
Razor-billed curassow	Paujil	Bung	*Mitu tuberosum*
Scarlet macaw	Guacamayo	Uhmay	*Ara macao*
Spix's guan	Pucacunga	Parund	*Penelope jacquacu*
Tinamou	Perdiz	Cognpo	*Tinamus guttatus*
Toucan	Tucán	Shirocwen	*Ramphastos cuvieri*

Figure 4. Spix's guan (*Penelope jacquacu*)

Figure 3. Collared peccaries (*Tayassu tajacu*)

Figure 5. Tapir (*Tapirus terrestris*)

The presence of animals near the agricultural fields is irregular. Instead of waiting for them to appear, people who wish to hunt have better chances of finding game in the forest, especially near saltlicks. Saltlicks are located several miles away from the community. Men in the community of Queros also use hunting trails that take them through places where animals feed or pass through, according to the season.

Around the middle of the twentieth century, the Wachiperi used to hunt frequently during the day. While using the moon and lanterns as the only sources of illumination worked for fishing, they were not good enough for hunting, except in the case of armadillos. More recently, the greater availability of flashlights allowed Wachiperi men to go hunting at night as often as during the day. The time it takes them to hunt varies. During the day, they usually go on short trips to the forest, which take between three and six hours. Today, most of these hunting trips are unproductive in terms of meat acquisition, since people who go hunting usually return to the community empty-handed. This low productivity is one of the reasons why people in Queros have been spending more time in nocturnal hunting than in hunting activities during the day.

Regarding nocturnal hunting, trips usually last all night, since people who go hunting at night build temporary tents by the riverbanks and usually sleep there. In terms of meat acquisition, nocturnal hunting is reported to be slightly more productive than hunting during the day, especially when it comes to finding small animals like armadillos. Nocturnal hunting also requires less physical effort than hunting during the day.

This type of hunting is also considered a form of recreation for men, since obtaining game is sometimes reported to be less important than their nocturnal hunting experience. People usually wait in tents for animals to show up, chewing coca leaves and enjoying the peaceful environment of the riverbanks at night. They often remain silent to avoid being detected by animals. Individuals fond of hunting tend to do it about three times per week, usually combining nocturnal hunting with hunting activities during the day. Most people in the community of Queros who hunt on a regular basis are men falling within the range of twenty-five to fifty years old.

Though hunting activities among the Wachiperi were normally conducted by men, an exception I found was the case of a woman in the community who hunted armadillos in the forest. She went hunting in the company of her dogs, who she said taught her how to hunt. After deciding to go hunting, she called her dogs, gathered up a machete and a lantern, and went into the forest. During her trips to the forest, she discovered that when armadillos took refuge in their holes, it was easier to push them out by introducing an irritating plant called *shiipi* or *soleman* into their hiding places, which caused armadillos to feel uncomfortable inside their holes. When they emerged she was waiting by the entrance of the hole and hit them with a machete. She conducted this activity in areas of the forest near the village, usually no more than half an hour away. The main reason she started hunting was to have meat to feed her children after her husband died. This woman also taught her daughter how to hunt armadillos, and the daughter in turn transmitted this knowledge to her two daughters. However, none of them adopted hunting as a regular activity. The daughter was usually busy conducting both subsistence and commercial agriculture, and the granddaughters moved to Pillcopata to attend secondary school.

While the behavior of this female hunter followed a different pattern than the one of male hunters, who at that time preferred to hunt larger animals in the forest farther away from the community during the day, both men and women in the community also considered her activities as hunting. The use of the Wachiperi term for hunting (*emasonka*) applied to both armadillo hunting and the typical hunting style with bow and arrow or shotgun, and did not imply male exclusiveness. Nevertheless, female hunting was not a common activity. Hunting was a social role women were not expected to perform. However, if women decided to hunt, there were no social restraints or means of social control in place that prevented them from openly pursuing this activity, like myths of taboos found in other places. Regarding the limited participation of women in hunting, the main restraint I perceived was women's limited hunting knowledge. In previous decades women were not taught how to hunt, a factor that discouraged them from pursuing this activity since their productivity was expected to be low.

Other women in the community also killed animals on certain occasions, such as when going to their agricultural fields in search of cassava or when walking by the riverbanks. Once, a woman from Queros went to the river to catch catfish and suddenly encountered a paca swimming slowly in her direction. She killed it with her machete right away. However, since the original goal of her trip was not to hunt animals, and killing pacas was not conducted in a systematic or recurrent way, this type of circumstantial animal killing was not considered hunting by most Wachiperi, both men and women. It was only considered a fortunate but circumstantial event. Even the woman who killed the animal described the event as "only one time, not always."

Despite the fact that hunting was a practice conducted mostly by men, Wachiperi women also played an important role in this activity. Until the middle of the twentieth century, there were cases when women and their children sometimes joined their husbands on trips to the forest in search of game. As a man of Queros described it, "Women sometimes accompanied their husbands when they went on long trips of two days, but not when they only went for one day."

The company of women allowed men to travel farther into the forest. When the hunt was successful, women helped carry the dead animals back to their houses. If a man went to the forest by himself and hunted more than one animal in a place far from his house, he had to dispose of parts of the animals, decreasing their weight to the amount he was able to carry by himself. This was not an ideal situation, since it reduced the amount of food available for consumption and distribution. However, for the most part it was just men who went hunting, since women had other activities to perform. As an elderly woman from Queros recalled, "When men went hunting, women stayed cooking, doing laundry, cleaning the agricultural field." Nowadays, women do not join their husbands when they go hunting. When a man hunts a large animal, he comes back to the community and invites others to help him bring the animal to the village. As a person from Queros described it, "Let's say I hunted a tapir, then I come to the community carrying a leg and tell others to come help me carry the remaining parts of the animal, and the ones who want to do it quickly get ready and go with me to bring the meat to the village." When asked if the meat would stay safe or if other animals would eat the meat in his absence, this hunter replied, "It is possible but not likely; jaguars kill their own animals and do not touch the ones we hunt, and we do the same for them."

Another area where women participated in the hunting process was the butchering and distribution of the meat obtained. Once hunters brought the meat of large animals to their houses and cut it down into large pieces, it was generally the women who took care of slicing the meat into smaller pieces and carrying out the distribution among relatives and friends. Men also participated in the distribution decisions, especially when other hunters were present in the party who were unable to kill animals for themselves. In some cases, animals were also butchered and divided into pieces in the place where they were hunted, and a quick distribution of the meat took place on the spot. However, once the killed animals reached the village, it was mainly the women who performed the distribution and cooking of the meat. Distribution decisions were based on participation in the hunting trip, reciprocity, kinship, friendship, and number of people in the recipient's household, among other criteria. These practices are still maintained today, even though the distribution of meat is minimal, since the availability of meat for distribution has decreased in the last decades. The practice of sharing food products has declined as well. This trend started when a few individuals stopped sharing the meat of the animals they hunted, creating a similar reaction among the others. As a man from Queros stated, "Once someone breaks the sharing pattern, then everyone starts doing the same." Growing scarcity of available meat as a result of less hunting also contributed to a reduction in their distribution practices.

The participation of women in hunting by joining hunting parties and performing tasks complementary to hunting, like butchering, distributing, and cooking the meat, illustrates the important role of women in activities dominated by men. However, women's contributions in Wachiperi society were for the most part not regarded with the same level of importance as men's activities. This situation reflects a system of gender stratification, which evaluates the roles of men and women and attributes statuses in unequal ways (Mascia-Lees and Black 2000: xii).

The circumstances surrounding hunting described here refer mainly to times of peace, but in the past there were also times of conflict, which created their own set of priorities. Conflicts were frequent among the different Harakmbut groups, and these were engaged in mainly by men. Some women also participated in the conflicts, mainly in activities such as cooking for the warriors and caring for the wounded. According to an elderly woman from Queros, "Fearful women did not go, they stayed in their houses, but brave women followed and accompanied their husbands to battle."

Other Subsistence Activities

Hunting in the Amazon region is normally combined with other subsistence activities, especially agriculture (Holmberg 1969: 67). Among the Wachiperi, agricultural plots were considered the property of the family that cultivated it, involving women and men. As Califano describes, men and women identified the optimal area for the establishment of a new plot. Men slashed the trees and burned them to clear the field. Women sowed the seeds and conducted the harvest, usually enlisting the help of other female neighbors and relatives (Califano 1982: 85–87). After the field was created, women undertook most of the routine agricultural work, providing a regular influx of food to their households.

The main agricultural species traditionally cultivated by the Wachiperi were cassava, bananas, papaya, beans, wild potatoes, barbasco, pineapple, sweet potatoes, sugarcane, maize, cotton, achiote, chili pepper, coca leaves, and tobacco. Plantain and peachpalm trees were also commonly cultivated, especially around the borders of the fields. The main plant species brought by outsiders to the region included rice, coffee, guava, and squash, in addition to new varieties of corn, bananas, cassava, and sugarcane (Califano 1982: 89–90). These crops were likely introduced by plantations in the area and via exchanges with other indigenous groups. The Wachiperi also prepared *masato* (*shiine*), a beverage made out of cassava, which sometimes was left to ferment to produce an alcoholic beverage for festive occasions. As Lyon explained in detail, masato drinking parties were an important part of the Wachiperi culture, since they allowed the release of internal social tensions and the resolution of conflicts (1967: 74).

Fishing was another important source of protein in the subsistence practices of indigenous peoples in the Amazon region. Around the middle of the twentieth century, Wachiperi men fished with arrows. There were two types of arrow points designed to shoot fish, *hecpa* for medium-sized fish and *cuchiheypo* for small fish. Big fish were not caught by the Wachiperi, because most rivers in the area have shallow waters. Women also used to collect small catfish, which usually dwell under rocks by the riverbanks. Capturing catfish did not require any special tool, but it did require strength to move the rocks and skill to grab the fish before they swam away.

Another common fishing practice was based on group expeditions, which included men and women working together. They first went to a part of the river where fish were abundant and then constructed a small dam to concentrate the fish in a single place. Once the dam was built, they submerged the roots of the plant *kumo* (*Lonchocarpus sp.*), also known as *barbasco*, in the water. This plant made fish drowsy and float to the surface, allowing people to collect them in bags and baskets. These expeditions were undertaken especially in the dry season, when the new fish had reached optimal sizes. Around the middle of the twentieth century, fishing trips were also conducted on special occasions, like weddings and other parties. In these cases, men did not need to go hunting to obtain a source of animal proteins, since people who went fishing usually captured plenty of fish that kept all members of the community well fed.

Shortly after the establishment of permanent relations with members of Western society, the fish populations of the rivers near Queros became quickly depleted. This happened mainly because people in the area started using dynamite for fishing, an unsustainable harvesting technique. As the Baptist missionary Robert Whatley explained to me in a personal communication, in the 1960s the Wachiperi started using dynamite to fish in the rivers of the area. They obtained the dynamite from police officers in Pillcopata and fished with it following the example of settlers. In a few years, this created a scarcity of fish that remains until today, even though the Wachiperi stopped using dynamite several decades ago. The main fishing tool currently used is fishing hooks. Now they have even adopted a defensive attitude toward the scarce fish left in the rivers, reflecting an adaptive learning process (cf. Berkes 2004: 629; Berkes and Folke 1998: 10). However, the residents of Pillcopata and other nearby settlements keep coming to areas near Queros to fish with dynamite (*taquear* in the local Spanish). The direct effect of dynamite on keeping fish populations low is evident for the people of Queros. Fishing with dynamite is difficult to control because it is only done occasionally and at a micro level. On one occasion when I was traveling with the Wachiperi, we spotted from the road the silhouette of two people who seemed to be fishing with dynamite. It was around five o'clock in the morning and still dark. A woman from Queros went to confront them, but as soon as the fishers saw someone coming their way, they quickly packed up their belongings and ran into the forest.

Moments later, we heard them driving away on a motorcycle, the preferred means of transportation used by furtive fishers.

Gathering food products in the forest was another productive activity, which was mainly practiced by women. Occasionally men also gathered products in smaller amounts. Gathering included plant products such as palm cores and a wide range of tropical fruits. Animals were also collected, especially edible worms, river snails, bird eggs, and frogs. Some of the products gathered were materials like the bark of some trees used to make elaborate bags, bamboo stems to make elaborate tools, and other substances used as ink for handicrafts. Another reason Wachiperi men and women collected forest products was for healing purposes, especially in the case of medicinal plants.

Trading was another activity practiced mostly by Wachiperi men. Around the middle of the twentieth century, they typically exchanged forest products, including colored feathers and animals intended to be sold as pets. These included macaws, parrots, monkeys, and other animals. Other products exchanged were coca leaves, bows and arrows, and fruits from the forest. In colonial times, some Wachiperi men made exchange trips to plantations, especially the ones run by people who showed a friendly attitude toward them. According to the Wachiperi today, these exchanges were common but infrequent, since they were afraid of catching diseases transmitted by outsiders. Other activities conducted by men and women included bringing firewood for the hearth and building houses. Women conducted tasks that did not require heavy lifting.

Household chores among the Wachiperi were conducted mainly by women. This was mainly evident in the case of cooking. Men were expected to bring the meat of the hunted animals to the house, and it was the role of women to cook it. An exception was when men hunted heavy animals far away from the community. In these cases, men had to smoke the meat on a stick over a fire to prevent it from spoiling. In other cases, men butchered the animals in the forest, buried the animals' intestines in the ground to reduce weight, and carried the meat back to the community on their backs, handing it over to their wives or other female relatives upon arrival. If women were not in the house, the male hunter left the meat in the kitchen area and went to rest, usually engaging in conversation with others. Preparing the meat and cooking it together with other food products harvested or gathered by women, like cassava and fruits, were important steps in the process of getting the food ready for consumption.

Women also made baskets, small and medium-sized bags, clothing, and handicrafts, particularly collars and crowns. Other tasks conducted by women included making, washing, and repairing clothes for all the members of their households, doing the dishes, bringing light firewood from the river, looking after the children, cleaning their houses and front yards, and feeding domestic animals, among other activities.

Many of these tasks are still practiced by the women of Queros today. When they do laundry, for instance, women gather the dirty clothes of all people in their household and go to the river for a few hours, especially on sunny days. They bring along their small children when they are not in school. Women hand wash clothes by the riverbanks, taking some time to swim once the clothes are rinsed. Girls are expected to help their mothers do the laundry from the time they are toddlers, increasing their level of contribution as they grow up. Boys are expected to clean only themselves and play by the river, but as they become older they stop joining their mothers on laundry days. By the time they reach the pre-teen stage, boys have a greater level of independence than girls and do not have to join their mothers anymore. The main expectations for boys today are to remain clean and do their school homework. This differentiation in the social expectations for boys and girls is an example of a current key practice shaping and communicating gender roles among the Wachiperi.

Changes in Social Roles

In the middle of the twentieth century, relationships between Wachiperi men and women were more egalitarian than they are today. As reported by elder people from Queros, family decisions were mostly made by couples, and there was no tradition of authoritarian interactions between husbands and wives. Men and women also made decisions in their respective spheres of influence, the ones related to their social roles according to gender, as described in Table 2. Both husband and wife usually respected the decisions of their spouses. Separations among couples were rare, but a woman could abandon her husband and end the relationship without social punishment. According to Lyon, "It was considered her husband's duty to keep her contented so that she would not run away" (1967: 30). Cases of physical violence between men and women were also uncommon. Since households tended to host several nuclear families, disagreements among couples were usually witnessed or overheard by the other residents, providing a means of social control. When there were arguments between a couple, the elder members of the family advised both people, especially the ones who were deemed responsible for the quarrels, encouraging them to modify their behavior in a friendly and constructive way.

Wachiperi women also mention that relationships between men and women started to change when they increased their interactions with outsiders, especially with Andean immigrants. They describe the introduction of machismo as a situation where Wachiperi men followed the example of settlers. As a woman of Queros pointed out, "There was no machismo before, like the outsiders that say to their wives 'bring me that' or 'prepare water for me.' It was not like that before, both men and women served each other ... outsiders have taught us that, the ones who came from the Andean region." Attitudes based on male dominance were also introduced by Andean men who married Wachiperi women.

The nuclearization of the households that occurred around the same time also contributed to the establishment of more authoritarian relationships, when large houses with several families were replaced by smaller single-family homes. This change in residence patterns took away much of the social control mechanism provided by other members of the house, which had previously prevented the mistreatment of women. Afterwards, men increasingly aimed to make their opinions prevail over their wives' when they had an argument. Likewise, women in the community have experienced more domestic violence from men in the last two decades, especially when men are drunk, which was unusual around the middle of the twentieth century. This violent behavior was probably influenced by the prevalence of ideas legitimizing this behavior among the Andean population who settled in the Kosñipata Valley, which place men in a higher position than women in terms of social status and portrays domestic violence under the influence of alcohol as a common occurrence.

A higher rate of separations among couples in the last few decades has also placed women in a situation of greater vulnerability, especially when women are the ones abandoned, along with their young children. Economic problems have been reported by people of Queros as a source of conflict among couples and identified as an important cause of separations. Today, raising children has become an expensive activity, especially since their current upbringing requires investing in milk, clothing, diapers, school materials, toiletries, and other expenses. A census of the current population of the community revealed that more than one-third of the couples did separate after a few years of living together and usually after having some children as well. While both men and women have been able to find new suitable partners after splitting, the marital instability has increased the uncertainty of couples about the strength of conjugal relationships, affecting their levels of confidence about joint initiatives and long-term planning.

Influence of Gender on Hunting

Changes in gender relationships affected Wachiperi hunting practices in significant ways. In the middle of the twentieth century, Wachiperi women encouraged men to go hunting, providing a means of social control that ensured an adequate supply of food, especially meat. In the case of the Sharanahua, another indigenous group of Peru, Siskind wrote that "men face the ridicule of their wives if they return empty-handed" after their trips to the forest, treating them with coldness for the absence of meat even if there were other types of food available (1973: 233). While women's pressure was considerably less prominent among the Wachiperi, there was an implicit expectation for men to contribute meat to the nutritional needs of their families and households. This situation applied mainly to married men, but to a lesser extent also to unmarried adult men. Wives in particular expressed their desire to eat the meat of certain animals, encouraging their partners to search for them in the forest.

In the decades that followed, the greater availability of food options changed the expectations about the contributions of men, extending the range of valid alternatives to other food products, not necessarily meat. Today, the main expectation for men is to fulfill their role as providers, which can be done by bringing forest, market, or manufactured products to their households. Wachiperi society expects men to ensure an adequate supply of food for their families, regardless of the type of food or its source.

Beyond basic sustenance, there are also values associated with the type of food consumed. Manufactured and other products acquired in the market have been gradually placed on top of the list of people's preferences.[7] The main products the Wachiperi purchase now include canned fish,

---

[7] Food consumption is not only a nutritional act but also social one, loaded with subjective meanings and implications for self-perception and cultural identity. The type of food consumed is also an expression of acquisitive power.

noodles, rice, potatoes, milk, eggs, chicken, onions, tomatoes, carrots, and lentils. In contrast, traditional meals based only on cassava and the meat of forest animals have become less attractive to them. In practice, however, most of the Wachiperi diet today is a combination of cultivated and purchased food products. These changes in eating habits have mainly favored men, since the income-generating activities are conducted mostly by them. As a result, there is less pressure for women to encourage men to go hunting, so men focus instead on the acquisition of food in different ways. There is greater priority on income-generating activities, which enable people to purchase food but has also decreased the practice of subsistence activities like hunting.

Contemporary expectations of Wachiperi men to secure an adequate supply of food for their households are part of a process of livelihood diversification. The changes in the food consumption patterns of the Wachiperi include a higher number of food products purchased in the market. This situation reflects a trend among the Wachiperi to invest more time and energy in activities that can provide them with the means to purchase external food products and combine them with those that are locally produced or acquired. Accordingly, hunting has increasingly become an activity of lower concern among the Wachiperi. The decreased interest in hunting is as a process directly related to the emergence of alternative means of making a living in the context of a mixed economy, promoting new behaviors that have been defining a pattern.

Overall, the gendered division of labor among the Wachiperi has been very influential on their hunting practices. Around the middle of the twentieth century, the division of labor defined the social roles expected from men and women to ensure the subsistence of the group, encouraging men to learn how to hunt and to provide their families with a regular flow of meat. In the following decades, Wachiperi social roles and their associated gender relationships changed in a significant manner. The adoption of new gendered attitudes characterized by men's dominance were affected by macho practices assimilated from Andean immigrants, the nuclearization of

Wachiperi households, and the subsequent loss of the important means of social control provided by other family members present in the large houses they previously inhabited. Also influential were changes in food consumption, which increasingly defined a preference for products purchased in the market, and the diversification of livelihoods in the context of a mixed economy, which encouraged people to generate monetary income to satisfy their needs and desires for new foods. These changes had a direct effect on the hunting practices of the Wachiperi, since the social roles of men and women had to adapt to the new socioeconomic conditions. As a result of these changes, the intensity of Wachiperi hunting practices decreased, along with the social prestige associated with hunting, the ability and interest of women to pressure their husbands to go to the forest in search of game, and the consumption of the meat of forest animals in general.

This situation is consistent with the idea that the roles and positions of men and women in society depend on their economic relationships. However, it is also important to take into account the effect of race and ethnicity on gender relations (Mascia-Lees and Black 2000: 67), especially considering the different ethnic background of some Andean immigrant men who married Wachiperi women in the last two decades, who had different sets of expectations about gender relations.

Examining the role of both men and women in hunting was a rich area for exploration, not only in terms of their contributions toward the subsistence of the group, but especially in terms of the interactions between men and women. These interactions produced a set of mutual expectations leading to the fulfillment of their social roles in a complementary way, not as completely separate spheres.

The use of "alternate caretakers" who watched over children while their mothers conducted physical activities that required spending high levels of energy (Peacock 1991: 345) was a common practice among people from Queros. This practice, together with the participation of women in support of activities like hunting and logging, contributed to women's active participation in a variety of activities. A related point is that most productive activities among the Wachiperi are not individual enterprises but joint efforts in the household that included the participation of both men and women. These conditions support the position of Stange (1997), who argued that gender roles should be understood beyond oppositional associations, like the ones that portray men as hunters and women as gatherers, which tend to be misleading.

The effect of gender roles on hunting, together with the historical processes affecting hunting practices identified in Chapter One, provide a greater understanding of the different processes affecting hunting intensity. These conditions, however, are mainly related to the specific case of the Wachiperi, since the processes described here refer to their particular experience. To complement this analysis, it is also necessary to evaluate the extent to which additional factors, identified by researchers as influential in other geographical and cultural settings, contribute to explain the variation in the hunting practices of the Wachiperi. The next chapter adopts this analytical approach, assessing the applicability of cross-cultural factors in the case of the Wachiperi, broadening our understanding of the multiple influences shaping indigenous environmental behavior.

Chapter III

Contemporary Influences on Hunting

My work with indigenous peoples has taken me to a number of communities in the Peruvian rain forest. Each of the groups I have studied had their own characteristics, which made them different from each other in terms of histories, present lives, and expectations for the future. At the same time, there were also common patterns among them. In the case of indigenous environmental behavior, the existence of similar conditions across different indigenous groups suggests the need to evaluate the influence of these common factors in the contemporary hunting practices of the Wachiperi.

This chapter is a succinct exploration of the diverse factors affecting hunting intensity among indigenous peoples across different places and cultures. These factors include an array of material conditions, cultural attitudes, and structural processes identified as relevant in the review of the specialized literature. I examine the significance of each of these factors among the Wachiperi, assessing their actual influence on the ground. The chapter concludes with a synthesis of the most influential factors that directly contribute to the current hunting intensity levels among the Wachiperi.

An analytical approach that evaluates the relevance of cross-cultural factors in the case of the Wachiperi is important because oftentimes there is a tendency to favor a predefined set of factors in the analysis of environmental problems, based on personal beliefs or academic traditions. These explanations may or may not be adequate in different contexts, since the

69

social and environmental conditions may vary significantly across sites. As Vayda pointed out, research should avoid focusing on only one set of explanatory factors privileged in advance (2009: 12). Accordingly, analyses that adopt uniform sets of priorities in all cases are likely to be a poor match with the actual problems on the ground, especially as the levels of variation across sites increase. Based on these considerations, the following sections examine the influence of some cross-cultural factors on the intensity of Wachiperi hunting practices.

Material Conditions

This section addresses the influence of material conditions on the intensity of Wachiperi hunting practices, including ecological features, population trends, consumption levels, and technological availability.

Ecological Features

Queros is located in a section of wet tropical forest known as *selva alta* or upper rain forest. The altitude of Queros varies between 890 and 1,000 meters above sea level, which creates a climate that is usually warm and wet, with an average temperature falling between 70 and 100 degrees Fahrenheit and an average relative humidity of 80% (Pinasco 2002: 9; Contreras 2007: 5). There are two marked seasons, rainy and dry. The rainy season usually runs from November to April, and the dry season from May to October. However, in recent years people from Queros have been experiencing changes in local weather patterns, warmer in the dry season and rainier in the wet one, in addition to seasons being delayed for up to two months. This has affected several subsistence activities, especially agricultural cycles.

The community of Queros is located in the transition zone of the Manu Biosphere Reserve and in the buffer zone of Manu National Park, an area with a high concentration of biological diversity. This area is also located within the Vilcabamba-Amboró conservation corridor, which links protected areas in northwestern Bolivia with southeastern Peru. The renowned conservation biologist John Terborgh stated that "as a repository of biodiversity, the Manu stands without peer. Its location in the Western fringe of the Amazon basin puts it at the world's biodiversity epicenter" (Terborgh 2004: 23). This statement coincides with descriptions of elders of Queros that forest animals were abundant in the past.

Seasons have some effect on the intensity of hunting practices in Queros. Hunting activities are more frequent in the dry season, especially between May and October, but some hunting is also done in the rainy season. This is a result of game being more abundant during the dry season, or summertime, because many animals come to areas that are more accessible to people, like riverbanks and flatlands. This situation applies especially in the case of animals like paca, capybara, deer, and white-throated tinamou. In addition, summer is the mating season for many forest-dwelling animals, like peccaries, monkeys, pacas, deer, armadillos, and capybaras. As such, they are more likely to travel farther from their more reclusive dwelling spaces in search of mating partners. Hunting is less frequent in the rainy season in part because the trails turn muddy, making it more difficult for people to take long walks in the forest. However, the rainy season is also important for hunting. Animals like tapirs and peccaries come to feed from the ripe fruits of trees like aguaje (*Mauritia flexuosa*), especially between January and March. There are also animals that live in the forest throughout the year without significant seasonal changes in their behavior. Such animals include agoutis, toucans, spix's guans, and common piping guans. Accordingly, hunting is more frequent during the times and in the places where it is most likely for people to find game.

Presently, the availability of some forest animals has decreased. A survey of people's perceptions about the availability of forest animals I conducted in 2009 revealed that some animals are still abundant, especially armadillos, brown agoutis, monkeys, and birds. However, other animals like white-lipped peccary, deer, and capybara are increasingly scarce. Survey respondents attributed recent animal scarcity to the degradation of the forest due to activities like logging (68%), which is followed by disturbances in the forest, especially the loud noises produced by chain saws (27%) and the growth of the settlers' population in the surroundings of Queros (5%).

Activities related to hunting were not reported as a significant cause of animal scarcity. However, the scarcity of animals has contributed to a reduction in the frequency of hunting, since obtaining game has become considerably more difficult. Today, people need to make longer trips to the forest to increase their chances of finding game, and their return rates have decreased significantly in comparison to previous decades. The amount of effort that it takes to hunt scarce animals in some cases has become greater than the benefits obtained, especially when people return empty-handed from their trips to the forest, as is increasingly the case. In a survey about hunting practices I conducted in the community of Queros in 2008, people reported that at least half the time they returned empty-handed after trips to the forest in search of game. Thus the efficiency of hunting has decreased while the opportunity costs of this activity have increased.

Population Trends

According to elder members of Queros, the Wachiperi population living in the Kosñipata Valley in their grandparents' times numbered several hundred individuals, but contagious diseases like smallpox and violent conflicts wiped out most of them. As Pinasco wrote, the Wachiperi were decimated as a result of their interactions with outsiders, reducing the total Wachiperi population from about two hundred right before the middle of the twentieth century to about seventy people after the deaths from smallpox (2002: 13).

Previously, many Wachiperi had also died in violent encounters with other indigenous groups and in conflicts with the inhabitants of the plantations established in the area. Some of the surviving Wachiperi moved into a Baptist mission, where they constituted a group that ranged between twenty-five and fifty individuals at different points in time. Other Wachiperi families went to live with the Matsiguenka, where they later formed the community of Huacaria. Some went to live in the Catholic mission of Palotoa and later stayed in the community of Shintuya, where most of the population is Amarakaeri. At some point, the dispersion of the population placed the community of Queros in danger of disappearance, but recently the population has stabilized.

In 2009, the community of Queros consisted of sixty people. Of these, about half lived in the community on a full-time basis, in addition to a few people who also lived in Queros but were not members of the community. These external members were the school teacher and three students who lived in Queros when they attended school. About a third of the population of Queros lived in Pillcopata. Some individuals also resided in Cusco and other places. These people were considered members of Queros, even if they lived somewhere else. Students attending college in Cusco, for instance, were considered full members of the community, away on a temporary basis. The same situation applied to people working in other places. This residential dispersion defined the character of the community not as a territorially bounded unit, but mainly as a social network of people that transcended a single geographical space.

One of the main reasons people from Queros left their community in the past is reported to be because of limited income-generating opportunities. The establishment of interactions with Western society generated new needs that required the generation of income. These needs include new food products, clothing, toiletries, cleaning supplies, batteries for flashlights, children's expenses, and others that at the time could not be adequately satisfied by remaining in Queros. Thus leaving their community was a coping strategy for many Wachiperi. Another important factor for leaving the community is education. To attend secondary school, students must go to Pillcopata, and to attend college they must go to the city of Cusco. Parents struggle to make enough money to send their children to school outside the community. Many people from Queros found that they could not earn enough money living in Queros, so they decided to pursue new economic activities in other places, encouraging emigration. In 2004, the completion of an electricity project in Queros revived some hopes for retaining the village's population. This step was reinforced in 2008 by the improvement of the road from Queros to a point close to Pillcopata, which offered greater possibilities for selling agricultural products, acting as an economic incentive to keep people in the community. The existence of new projects with direct benefits for the population, like tourism and conservation, are also considered important factors that could help maintain or increase the population of Queros. This situation is a beneficial outcome resulting from the growth of their mixed economy, favoring the diversification of their livelihoods.

At current levels, the population density of Queros is about 2.5 people per square mile. This ratio indicates a very low level of demographic density, which is directly correlated with the current low levels of hunting among the Wachiperi. However, this does not imply the existence of a causal relationship, since other productive activities have been exploited in an increasingly intense way. These productive activities include fishing, timber harvesting, and agriculture. In addition, their low population density has not always been accompanied by low levels of pressure on forest animals, since some species have become increasingly scarce in the last decades. During the 1960s, the Wachiperi temporarily increased their levels of hunting intensity after the introduction of shotguns, even though their population was small at that time. Later on, the introduction of flashlights also helped increase the levels of nocturnal hunting. In addition, species were made scarcer because the Wachiperi are not the only ones living in the area, and people from neighboring places have been hunting forest animals for both consumption and trade.

Overall, the decline of the Wachiperi population created a significant reduction in the absolute levels of hunting in comparison to the time when they were more numerous, because fewer people need less game to feed themselves. As such, the decimation of the population decreased their levels of hunting in the following decades. However, on a per capita basis, population decline was especially relevant in terms of the deep social disruptions they created on Wachiperi society, but not because of a reduction in the size of the population per se. At this level, the greatest effects of population decline on hunting intensity were mostly qualitatively, not quantitatively determined. Moreover, the effects of population changes need to be understood in terms of their interconnections with other relevant factors beyond demographic trends, especially the settlement patterns that brought the Wachiperi together in the Baptist mission and the socioeconomic changes the Wachiperi experienced when they became engaged in market exchanges.

Consumption Levels

People from Queros currently consume a combination of both cultivated and purchased food products. The main cultivated products include cassava, bananas, beans, wild potatoes, peachpalm, sweet potatoes, plantains, and squash. Products bought in the market include rice, potatoes, chicken, lentils, and dried beef meat, along with manufactured products like noodles, canned tuna, salt, sugar, cheese, and others. A common dish in the community of Queros today (see Figure 6) is comprised of rice, noodles, potatoes, tomatoes, and pieces of meat. Although less frequent, forest products that are consumed include meat, fish, edible worms, and wild fruits, depending on the products available in each season. In the last two decades, discrimination against indigenous peoples due to their food consumption patterns has affected the Wachiperi's consumption of forest products. As a member of Queros recalled, classmates in the school of Pillcopata used to tease him with phrases like "frog eater" and "worm eater." This situation may have been influential in the food preferences of the Wachiperi at later stages of their lives, encouraging them to prefer non-stigmatized food options.

This situation has started to reverse, but mostly in a symbolic way. People from Queros sometimes consume forest foods as a mark of cultural identity and pride, which is increasingly recognized by people in Pillcopata. During the festivities for the 2009 anniversary of Kosñipata, a contest of local dishes was held. One prize went to a person from Queros who prepared a dish based on palm worms and plantains. This turn of events reflects a strategic essentialist approach to Wachiperi cuisine adopted by some people of Queros. However, this attitude is not constant, since most people in Queros currently consume products purchased in the market.

Acquisition of non-edible products by the Wachiperi is minimal. Most of the garbage produced in the community of Queros is made out of biodegradable components and food cans. The younger generation, however, displays different patterns of food consumption (see Figure 7), including a greater amount of secondary needs. However, most adults have not increased their amount of food consumption in significant ways, reflecting a situation where the changes in their food consumption patterns are mainly qualitative.

People in Queros eat their heaviest meals at breakfast and lunch. However, some people tend to skip meals, replacing lunch with early dinner. This pattern is common among people who spend all morning taking care of their agricultural plots and those who go to the forest to hunt or gather products. As a result, some of them have developed gastric problems that increasingly require medical attention.

Figure 6. Wachiperi man sharing a meal with his favorite pet

Figure 7. Child from Queros purchasing ice cream at the town fair

Food preferences vary among individuals, but according to a survey I conducted in 2009, most people from Queros prefer fish (52%). Others prefer the meat of forest animals (29%) or chicken (19%) as their favorite type of meat. In the case of forest animals, most Wachiperi prefer to eat paca, birds, tapir, and deer. Birds provide tastier meat but only in reduced amounts. Tapirs provide the greatest amount of meat, allowing its distribution among friends and relatives. Pacas provide a balance between taste and amount of meat, thus being the most sought after species. Deer are also highly appreciated, but finding them in the forest is rare today.

Most of the time, however, the preferences of people for these animals do not correspond to the actual animals hunted, since it turns out that armadillos are most frequently consumed by people in Queros. In a similar way, the scarcity of fish in the rivers of the area has resulted in people oftentimes resorting to canned food. As a Wachiperi person pointed out, "Before there were plenty of animals, we used to eat well, good fish fresh from the river, but now we have to eat tuna fish from a can."

There are special occasions when the expectations to obtain forest meat are stronger. The anniversary of the community creation in October and the carnival celebrations in February are the main occasions. In preparation for these festivities, the Wachiperi gather and designate hunting parties to obtain enough meat for everyone in the community, including guests from nearby settlements. These hunting parties leave Queros a few days in advance, walking to more distant points in the forest to increase their chances of obtaining enough meat in time for the festivities. Other occasions when people are asked to go hunting include receiving important community guests, such as top officials of their supporting organizations, donors funding the projects in Queros, and groups of tourists who visit the community.

Beyond designated hunting parties, regular consumption of the meat of forest animals has decreased in the last decades. Today, people from Queros only consume this type of meat about twice a month on average, and every two months in the case of the people from Queros living in

Pillcopata. However, this is only an approximate account, since there is considerable variation in the consumption of meat. For the most part, people from Queros reported that they eat the meat of forest animals "when it is available." This reduction in meat consumption is reinforced by changes in their food preferences, which place greater emphasis in the acquisition of food products acquired in the market. Thus reduced consumption of the meat of forest animals has affected hunting intensity, since the contemporary expectations for obtaining the meat of forest animals have become secondary to other available food alternatives.

Technological Availability

Until the middle of the twentieth century, the main hunting tools employed by the Wachiperi were bow and arrow. These were made by men, but women prepared the bowstrings. There were six major types of arrows, each designed to hunt specific animals, according to their size and type of habitat, as well as variants for each of these types. The Wachiperi word for the bow is *kumej*, and the generic name for arrows is *pija*. Some of their arrows were intended to catch fish. Figure 8 shows the types of arrows customarily used by the Wachiperi and their intended prey.

In the ancestral Wachiperi perceptions, the symbolic transference of attributes to hunting tools was also an important factor believed to influence their effectiveness. As Califano described, the fabrication of the arrows and their efficiency did not depend only on the technical qualities of their manufacture, but also on the power embedded in them via the procedure known as *eshuva*. This process involved gathering the arrows together, spitting and blowing on the arrow points, and singing to them while invoking the injuring properties of insects like hornets and bees, thus transferring the power of their stingers (Califano 1985: 11–12).

After moving to the Baptist mission in the 1950s, the Wachiperi quickly acquired shotguns. These new weapons created a temporary increase in their levels of hunting intensity, but in a few years they also contributed to a reduction in the amount of game available near their settlement. However, their frequency of hunting decreased again a few years after they adopted shotguns. The missionary Robert Whatley pointed out that in the 1960s it was already difficult for the Wachiperi to hunt. The missionaries initially provided the Wachiperi with some rifles in exchange for work. Shortly thereafter, the Wachiperi started acquiring shotguns directly from settlers in exchange for forest products. Afterwards, hunters continued using shotguns, even if they had to borrow them from someone else. At present, only two people from Queros own shotguns. Even if others are able to raise the money to purchase them, acquiring shotguns is no longer considered a priority investment among the Wachiperi.

Dogs were another important aid in the hunting process. For their training, dogs were taken for walks in the forest from the time they were pups so that they learned to feel comfortable moving in that environment. As the dogs grew, they were expected to help hunters find game. When dogs identified prey animals, like collared peccaries, they chased them until the escape routes were obstructed by some natural obstacle, like a steep hill or a hole, and then kept the prey animals cornered until the hunter arrived. In the case of animals that lived underground, such as armadillos, dogs were able to find and track them in their holes. Dogs also contributed to the safety of hunters, since they often identified and chased away dangerous animals like jaguars and snakes.

Today, hunting is done both day and night, depending on the game sought and the preferences of the hunter. The introduction of flashlights increased the frequency of nocturnal hunting, because the lanterns they had previously used were not very efficient means of illumination. Flashlights also contributed to reshaping hunting in a significant way, since it allowed hunters to identify some animals whose eyes reflect the light directed toward them in a distinguishable manner.

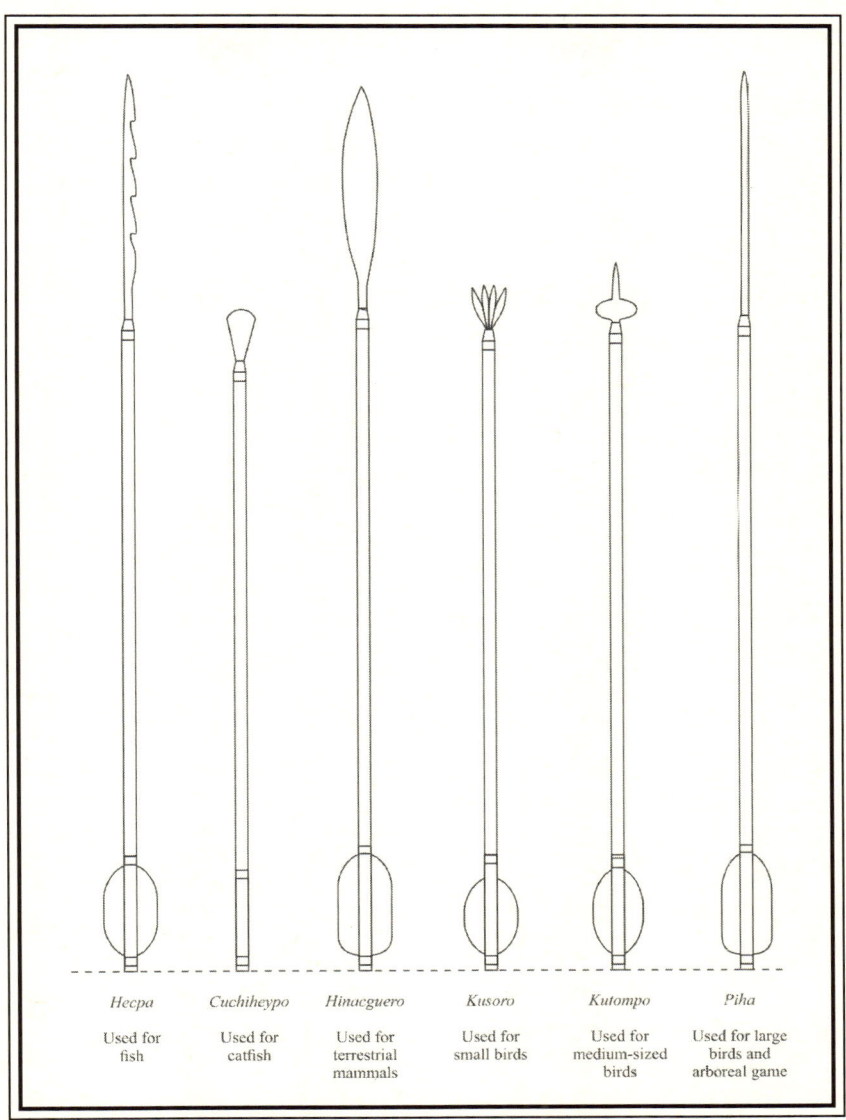

Heepa	*Cuchiheypo*	*Hinaeguero*	*Kusoro*	*Kutompo*	*Piha*
Used for fish	Used for catfish	Used for terrestrial mammals	Used for small birds	Used for medium-sized birds	Used for large birds and arboreal game

Figure 8. Types of arrows customarily used by the Wachiperi

The advantage of using flashlights increased in open areas like riverbanks, where the light was not obstructed by the presence of trees. Accordingly, the custom of going to the riverbanks in search of game during the night became more frequent while the practice of going to the forest started to decrease. This situation indicates that the introduction of flashlights increased the practice of nocturnal hunting. Nevertheless, nocturnal hunting has also been restricted by the limited availability of batteries to operate the flashlights, since a source of income is necessary to purchase them. Besides shotguns, dogs, and flashlights, people from Queros also took machetes, coca leaves, and cigarettes on their hunting trips to the forest or the riverbanks.

Overall, hunting technology produced important qualitative changes in the practice of hunting. Flashlights contributed to both a decrease in diurnal hunting and an increase in nocturnal hunting. Likewise, hunting activities decreased a few years after the introduction of shotguns, mainly as a result of the scarcity of game produced by a temporary increase in hunting when the Wachiperi moved into a single settlement and started hunting with shotguns. Accordingly, in the short term the introduction of new hunting technologies temporarily increased the intensity of hunting, but in the long term it also contributed to a scarcity of game near their settlement, which resulted in an overall reduction in the intensity of hunting practices among the Wachiperi to similar or lower levels than before the temporary increase.

Cultural Attitudes

This section considers the influence of cultural factors on the behavior of the Wachiperi, particularly how their perceptions of wildlife, spiritual beliefs about animals, moral values regarding hunting, and hunting knowledge have affected their hunting practices. In the ancestral Wachiperi cosmology, forest animals were perceived as beings that interacted with people, displaying patterns of thought and behavior similar to humans'. These interactions were framed in terms of conflict and war, typical of the Wachiperi society before the middle of the twentieth century. As Califano described, in a mythical tale the tapir is portrayed as a person that once plotted to kill the Wachiperi, but someone found out about his plans and killed the tapir first, turning the tapir into an animal. A similar tale describes how a Wachiperi warrior undertook a war against the jaguars as a form of revenge after they killed his mother. This was done with weapons made out of hard wood, acquired from a tree whose seeds he obtained with help from birds (Califano 1985: 11). These depictions reflect a situation where interactions with animals were addressed in similar ways to those with humans, deeply integrated into their cultural perceptions.

The spirits of the forest were perceived as entities reactive to the behavior of hunters. As Helberg described, the relationship between hunter and prey created a reciprocal effect, and the spirits of the animals could benefit or inflict harm on humans. These interactions happened mainly in the realm of dreams, where the spirits of the animals communicated with people. When people hunted in a respectful way, the spirits of the forest rewarded this behavior by sharing their knowledge about how and where to hunt. In cases where there was excessive hunting, animals could take actions to bring illnesses and even death to these hunters (Helberg 1996: 28). Thus perceptions of animals defined cultural limits aimed to prevent overhunting.

Wachiperi perceptions of wildlife are also reflected in their domestication of forest animals. In the middle of the twentieth century, they kept monkeys, tapirs, collared peccaries, capybaras, and different types of birds as pets. They had a close relationship with them. Even if they did not assign names to their pets, they were considered part of the family. The animals were captured at a young age and raised by the Wachiperi. Once these animals became used to the house and to being fed regularly, they were allowed to wander freely. Even today, many houses have parrots and macaws in addition to dogs and cats. Parrots are allowed on the dining tables and sometimes even eat from the same plates as their owners, as illustrated in Figure 6. When parrots reach adulthood and meet other members of their species who come to the area, they tend to bond with them and set off with their new partners, abandoning their houses and saddening their human owners. This behavior illustrates that forest animals are held in high regard and perceived as sentient living beings.

In the last few decades, the ancestral perceptions of animals have been increasingly forgotten by the new generation of young people, displaced by knowledge acquired in school and closer interactions with outsiders. While the ancestral view is still influential in how they understand the forest and its inhabitants, in many cases these perceptions have been challenged by more pressing concerns. These concerns refer to the need for money to cover basic needs while gradually introducing an alternative vision of natural resources based on their material benefits. These two visions have coexisted, but the materialistic view is becoming increasingly influential. In the case of hunting, the introduction of a material perception is reducing the value of forest animals to the benefits their meat can provide. Thus changes in the Wachiperi perceptions of wildlife have also been influential in reducing the intensity of their hunting practices.

These changes are recent. Until the middle of the twentieth century, people were expected to keep a good relationship with the spirits of the forest by showing respectful behavior toward them. According to Wachiperi elders, when they went to the forest, they had to ask the spirits of the animals for permission to kill some game first, and they could only ask for enough meat for purposes of subsistence. These spirits were called *Numberi, Wameri,* and *Oteri.* Numberi was the spirit ruling the forest and its inhabitants, especially animals. Wameri was the spirit of the river, which controlled fish and gave people the ability to differentiate between truth and lies, good and bad, so they could have good judgment, self-knowledge, and peace of mind in their lives. Oteri was the spirit of the mountains and the air, which controlled the higher parts of the hills, allowing living beings to breathe and live. The Wachiperi were placed in the middle of these spiritual entities and were expected to maintain a good relationship with them. These beliefs influenced their use of natural resources to maintain a social, environmental, and spiritual balance with the spirits of the forest. This balance also reflected a broad idea of sustainability, which added a spiritual dimension to their social and ecological interactions.

All species of forest animals that were important for Wachiperi subsistence had their own spirit protectors. These spirits inhabited the bodies of animals that were larger than average in size. These animals were expected to lead the other members of their species and protect them from danger. They were addressed with the term *wantopa*, which refers to the leader of a group. If permission from these spirits was granted to hunters in the dream world, hunters were allowed to take a few individuals of that species at a time. These spirit protectors sometimes talked to people when they were asleep, and even showed people the places where they could easily find prey. Chief among these spirits was the one of the jaguar, who had more power over the rest of the animals and was therefore an influential spiritual figure. This predator adopted the role of punisher for people who conducted inappropriate hunting practices, representing a threat in both the spiritual and the physical world. The physical threat was directly related to the exposure of hunters in the forest to potential jaguar attacks.

In the spiritual realm, failure to maintain a good relationship with the animal spirits was considered an invitation to trouble. People who hunted beyond their needs or without asking for proper permission were likely to infuriate the spirits of the forest. One of the typical forms of showing their displeasure was through illnesses sent to the hunter or his children, a process known as *dingaehe* or *cutipado*. The main ailments were diarrhea and vomiting, illnesses that started in the spiritual realm but whose implications reached the material world. Another form of punishing excessive or disrespectful hunting behavior was to send nightmares, troubling the sleep of hunters until they corrected their behavior. This act was known as *embayoroga* by the Wachiperi.

From a gendered perspective, spiritual beliefs were also ways of inscribing the value of hunting and therefore male power by surrounding hunting with ritual and taboo, especially considering that women's activities were not ritualized in similar ways. Lyon reported that Wachiperi myths did not focus on agriculture or agricultural products. By contrast, there were plenty of myths surrounding forest animals, which therefore attributed greater importance to hunting (Lyon 1967: 72). Since agriculture was one of the main activities conducted by women, as was hunting by men, the practical value of the tasks each gender performed were related to their symbolic value.

In recent decades, the pressure to cope with economic needs has become a more urgent concern, diverting the attention of the Wachiperi toward income-generating activities. However, the fact that people from Queros do not sell the meat of the animals they hunt indicates that their beliefs about forest animals have exerted an influence on their selection of economic alternatives. This behavior is also part of their sense of cultural identity, since the practice of not selling the meat of forest animals differentiates them from their non-indigenous neighbors. Accordingly, the spiritual beliefs of the Wachiperi also played a role in decreasing the intensity of hunting among them. When facing the requisite of income to satisfy their new needs, the Wachiperi choose to pursue activities that do not have strong spiritual beliefs preventing their commercial exploitation, such as agriculture and logging. As a person from Queros stated, among the Wachiperi "there has never been the idea of going to the forest to hunt an animal with the intention of selling it later."

Before the increased contact between the Wachiperi and outsiders in the middle of the twentieth century, Wachiperi traditions also included rules and restrictions to guide the practice of hunting based on the teachings of their ancestors. One of these rules applied to the classification of animals as edible and inedible, defining certain animals that should not be hunted and their meat always avoided. An example is the spectacled bear (*Tremarctos ornatus*). According to a mythical tale collected by Califano, the Wachiperi used to hunt bears that came to eat the seeds of their *pijuayo* trees (*Bactris gasipaes*), until one day they killed the chief of the bears and ate his meat. Afterwards, everyone who ate the meat of this bear got a terrible stomachache, and their bellies swelled until they exploded. Only the few people who did not eat that meat survived to tell the story (Califano 1985: 13).

These inherited values may explain why even today the Wachiperi do not hunt spectacled bears, since they consider their meat inedible. Other animals in this category include jaguars and other wild cats, giant anteaters, opossums, bamboo rats, and snakes, among others. In the case of jaguars and other wild cats, the Wachiperi do not eat them or kill them unnecessarily. As long as these forest predators do not attack people or their domesticated animals, they are left alone, even if their footprints are sometimes found in the vicinity of Queros. In a similar way, the Wachiperi do not take advantage of animals killed by wild cats. They believe that the meat belongs to the hunter, in this case the wild cats, and try to quickly leave the place where the animal was killed by the predator. This behavior is a way of showing respect for the right of others to feed themselves, as well as avoiding the possibility of making hungry wild cats angry.

Around the middle of the twentieth century, sharing the meat of hunted game was also an important part of the Wachiperi values associated with hunting. This practice reinforced the social links between hunters and other people in the community, as well as the relationship between family groups. Hunting was also a source of social prestige among the Wachiperi. The ability to provide an adequate supply of meat to their households was an important attribute among men and also allowed hunters to accumulate debts of gratitude and influence among the other members of the group.

In the last few decades, however, the relevance of hunting to social life has decreased, even if the ancestral values have not been completely forgotten. The interactions of the Wachiperi with Western society have generated the adoption of new values, including their desire to obtain a better education for their children, greater profitability to cover their basic needs, improved roads to facilitate their transportation, and improved communications, especially radio and television. These new values have gained predominance in the expectations of people from Queros. Thus the loss of relevance of their ancestral values has been associated with a decrease in the intensity of their hunting practices as a parallel process motivated by changes in their way of life.

Knowledge about the behavior of animals in the forest has been another important factor influencing the hunting practices of the Wachiperi. Hunting involves multiple skills related to finding animals in the forest, the ability to understand indicators of their proximity, and the capacity to apply this information in practice. As Califano described, there was a whole set of empirical knowledge related to the practice of hunting among the Wachiperi, like identifying the footprints of animals, the season and time when animals could be found, the smell they left in the forest, the insects that inhabited some animals and indicated their proximity, and the sounds animals made and their imitation by hunters, among others (Califano 1982: 88). Calculating the distance of animal sounds, the freshness of their footprints, and the direction of the wind were also important factors.

Learning the interactions between different species in the forest is another important skill for hunting. For instance, this skill is used in identifying the fruits of some forest trees that peccaries and tapirs like to eat. Accordingly, people go to the areas where these fruits are common, increasing their chances of finding game. Another example is the case of *shiwit*, a bird that usually follows jaguars in the forest. Hearing this bird singing is an indicator that a jaguar is present in the area. Knowing these associations between animals and identifying them accurately improves the chances of people who go hunting to find game and to remain safe in the forest.

Acquiring hunting knowledge involves a long process of learning, which implies a close familiarity with the forest ecosystem. People who hunt are expected to know the places where each species of animals stay according to the time of the year, their common feeding grounds, saltlicks, and routes of displacement. They need to know that strong body smells and even low noises make animals feel the presence of people, which causes them to run away to avoid humans. People who hunt also know that they do not have much time before the animals sense them, so they have to approach animals hiding behind obstacles and act quickly to avoid being discovered. Beginning around the middle of the twentieth century, male children were taken to the forest from an early age to learn these skills. Walking in the forest was part of a learning experience that allowed children to develop a sense of geographical orientation, overcome the feelings of strangeness in the forest, and identify the sounds of the forest. Boys continued this learning process until they reached adulthood. Even then, they had to continue learning to improve their effectiveness, finding their own style according to their household needs for meat and their personal preferences regarding the type of animals they liked to eat.

Nowadays the transmission of hunting knowledge has been severely disrupted. A survey I conducted in 2008 among people from Queros revealed that there is great variability in the age at which people went hunting for the first time, displaying a wide range from ten to forty years old, with an average of twenty-one when they first started hunting. This age is very late for people to start learning how to hunt, reducing their chances of becoming proficient hunters.

In the last few decades, significant parts of the Wachiperi's knowledge about hunting have been abandoned, affecting the hunting skills of the younger generations. From the time they went to live in the Baptist mission, children were expected to spend at least two hours per day listening to the missionary's preaching, reducing young boys' available time to join their fathers during hunting trips. After leaving the mission, the community started an elementary school that kept children busy. They were still able to go on hunting trips but on a less frequent basis because they had other concerns.

As a result of these changes in their way of life, many young people focused on pursuing a formal education, so their interest in learning how to hunt became less relevant in their daily lives. The achievements of educated people were also influential in terms of defining new role models, like Alejandro Jahuanchi, a Wachiperi who was trained as a teacher. His education provided him with knowledge that allowed him to lead the process of obtaining community lands for the Wachiperi. Thus when young people tried to go hunting after spending several years in school, the lack of knowledge about hunting made it difficult for them to be successful, turning their hunting efforts into fruitless enterprises and discouraging them from further attempts at hunting as a regular activity. Accordingly, the loss of hunting knowledge associated with their school duties had a direct effect in reducing the intensity of Wachiperi hunting practices.

Structural Processes

This section examines the influence of structural processes on the intensity of Wachiperi hunting practices, including market demands, unequal access to resources, regulatory frameworks, and diversification of livelihoods.

Market Demands

The demand for products from the Kosñipata Valley has been increasing in the last decades, following improvements in the conditions of the road from Pillcopata to Cusco. The main products in demand are timber and agricultural crops, especially cassava, rice, and coca leaves. The majority of the non-indigenous population in the area focuses on agriculture and logging. Ecotourism is another growing activity in

Pillcopata, which has created the need for new services for visitors, like restaurants and hostels. Tourism is supported by the transit of people on their way to Manu National Park, an area with high biological diversity. In the last years, the harvesting of butterflies has also attracted the attention of a growing number of people. Butterflies are captured for export to international markets.

The harvesting agents in the area are mainly small and independently owned operators, who sell their products to middlemen. Some people with enough financial resources make a living from buying and selling products like timber and butterflies while agricultural products are sold to truck owners or traders. In the case of coca leaves, there is an illegal network of buyers, following a similar process of middlemen agents. The exception is the case of ecotourism, where a consortium of travel agencies from Cusco (Ecoturmanu) dominates the market. It is significant that corporate agents common in other parts of the Peruvian rain forest, such as big mining, oil, and logging companies, are not present in the Kosñipata Valley.

The demand for the meat of forest animals in the local and regional market is small. Most of the population in the Kosñipata Valley consists of former Andean immigrants, who do not customarily eat the meat of forest animals. Even if some of them have eaten the meat of forest animals at some point, they see it as something foreign. Many settlers even look at this type of meat with disdain, joking about it as a less than ideal food choice. The exception is the paca (*Agouti paca*), whose tasty meat is increasingly considered an acceptable food choice, but its consumption is low because the price of this type of meat is high in comparison to the meat of other forest animals. The main destinations for the meat of forest animals are the restaurants in Pillcopata. As a result, paca is the only animal whose meat is commonly offered in restaurants, and the main consumers are tourists and traders.

In the case of Queros, people do not sell any of the meat from the animals they hunt. Their involvement in the market is limited to other activities, like selling agricultural products and

small amounts of timber. Some Wachiperi who live in
Pillcopata also conduct small-scale commercial activities, like
selling groceries or beverages for breakfast. As a result, the
demands of the regional market do not seem to have had a
direct influence on the intensity of hunting among the
Wachiperi. In an indirect way, market demands have drawn
people's attention away from hunting and toward other
income-generating activities like agriculture, small-scale
logging, trade, tourism, and paid environmental conservation
to satisfy their new needs and desires, creating a greater
diversification in their community livelihoods, which will be
discussed in the next chapter.

Access to Resources

Access to resources in the Kosñipata Valley is mainly
related to the distribution of land. Following an agrarian
reform in Peru during the 1970s, most lands surrounding
Pillcopata were allocated to different owners. Former
plantation employees acquired the plantation's lands, which
were divided among the workers and titled as private
property. Indigenous groups became Native Communities and
obtained collective lands. Most of the remaining lands were
granted as concessions, especially in the last decade. These
concessions are agreements between the Peruvian government
and the organizations that requested their administration for
different purposes. The normal period for these concessions is
forty years, to be administered according to management plans
that ensure their environmental sustainability. The first
concessions were given for the sustainable harvesting of
timber, and later on concessions were also granted for
ecotourism and biodiversity conservation. Accordingly, most
lands in the area are now controlled by a combination of small
land owners and concession users.

Nevertheless, land is not available for everyone. A large
number of young people, especially the descendants of Andean
migrants who settled in the Kosnipata Valley, now face

challenges finding productive land, particularly for agriculture and logging. This scarcity of land created a social movement of landless youth, the *Asociación de Jóvenes sin Tierras en Acción*. In June 2009, more than seven hundred people had joined this movement and planned to invade the lands they perceived as "unproductive," especially those areas with undisturbed forests. Areas targeted included government lands, conservation concessions, and also protected areas like the Amarakaeri Community Reserve, which is managed by a group of Native Communities. In July 2009, they invaded the lands of a government organization.

The squatters' approach was to take over lands that they perceived as unproductive. For instance, they perceived conservation concessions as a strategy of international interests to take over their natural resources by manipulating the indigenous communities of the area. However, squatters' plans did not consider the environmental sustainability of the area. Their concerns focused on short-term economic activities, like timber harvesting and agricultural expansion. Accordingly, in the Kosñipata Valley landless people are more likely to affect the area's biodiversity, while landowners and concessionaires are the ones more likely to protect it.

The allocation of land in this area is not directly related to the distribution of wealth, since landowners and concession holders are mainly people with low levels of income, in many cases barely struggling to pay the government fees for the use of the concession lands. This situation happens because income levels in the region are relatively low for everyone, without significant levels of economic differentiation. In the case of settlers, most lands were granted as part of an agrarian reform in the 1970s.

In a similar way, access to political power is a contested terrain, without an elite group that controls this process. Access to local government positions has been heavily contested, especially between people from the towns of Pillcopata and Patria. Social movements have also been influential, such as in the case of the *Frente Único de Defensa de los Intereses de*

Kosñipata, an association of loggers and producers of coca leaves. They aim for the lifting of restrictions to harvesting imposed by the government, and were successful in having one of their members elected as mayor of Pillcopata. Thus political power is not concentrated in a few influential people but is a contested space wherein people can gain temporary access according to the changing political circumstances.

The community of Queros has its own territory and also holds the Haramba conservation concession, which will be further discussed in Chapter Four. This situation allows them access to natural resources, and they are working toward safeguarding the biological diversity of this area from external threats, especially from loggers, butterfly catchers, and squatters who might potentially seek to invade the conservation concession land. In relation to hunting, the role of people from Queros has focused on keeping away hunters coming from neighboring places into both their community lands and concession area. The emergence of a greater need to conduct surveillance activities to conserve the natural resources in the lands under their control has also decreased their availability of free time, contributing to a reduction in their frequency of hunting, as discussed in the next chapter.

Regulatory Frameworks

Before territorial concessions, national legislation regarding the allocation of government lands granted rights of possession to people who conducted productive activities within them. Since the evidence of productive activities was expected to be visible, there was an incentive for people to clear down parts of the forest and create agricultural fields and later turn these areas into pastures for cattle. This system of perverse incentives was common until the late 1990s, when a new national policy was put in place. The new criteria was to allocate large areas of land as concessions, where the state retained legal ownership of the land but granted its use to qualified organizations, according to management plans intended to ensure the environmental sustainability of the area.

Currently the Peruvian legislation regarding forest animals is mainly contained in the *Ley Forestal y de Fauna Silvestre* N° 27308, introduced in 2000, which replaced the Decreto Ley N° 21147 and the Decreto Supremo 158-77-AG that previously regulated hunting activities in the country. The figure of concessions was one of the main features of Law N° 27308, including timber, non-timber products, ecotourism, conservation, and environmental services. In 2008, an attempt was made to replace Law N° 27308 with *Decreto Legislativo* N° 1090 and others. However, these new legal instruments were severely criticized by indigenous groups from the Amazon region, who started a series of road blockings as a measure of protest. In June 2009, dozens of indigenous peoples were killed by the police during an attempt to clear the roadblocks. This event captured the attention of many individuals and civil society organizations, creating national and international pressure on the government to avoid further use of violence against indigenous peoples. As a result, shortly after the killings the national government backed down on their attempts to have the new laws prevail, initially suspending them and later abolishing the new laws.

One of the main legal dispositions related to wildlife is that indigenous communities are able to conduct subsistence hunting activities inside their territories but not sell their meat. The only part of forest animals legally authorized to be sold is their skin. A person may hunt forest animals for their skin only after obtaining a license and within certain annual limits. Trading forest animals as pets is also prohibited, but non-indigenous persons oftentimes smuggle them. In the case of the Wachiperi, hunting activities were usually conducted in a manner consistent with the provisions of this law, since it coincided with their ancestral customs. Consequently, the national laws had little effect on the way they conducted their hunting practices.

In the community of Queros, the regulatory means are constituted mainly by internal community agreements. In the case of fishing, for example, several decades ago they agreed to stop fishing with dynamite, and that resolution is still maintained today. Logging is another activity where community agreements establish limits on the harvesting of timber. These limits are being reduced in a progressive way, as people from Queros move forward with their new community-based conservation agenda. In the case of hunting, however, there are no internal agreements because people in the community consider there to be no need for them. Since hunting is now done on a very small scale, involving only few people and without any visible impact on the availability of animals as a result of their hunting activities, it was not necessary to impose restrictions on this activity. Accordingly, the influence of regulatory frameworks on the intensity of hunting among the Wachiperi has been minimal, indicating that their hunting practices were affected mainly by other factors and processes.

Determining Local Relevance

Determining the relevance of local factors in environmental interventions and conservation strategies has in many cases been guided by preconceived notions associated with the disciplinary traditions and theoretical preferences of the researchers and practitioners involved. From a conservation biology perspective, scholars have argued that the definition of priority settings should be guided by factors like the number of endemic and total species, degrees of threat, population viability, ecological and evolutionary processes, and the economic costs and benefits of conservation (Lamoreux et al. 2007: 2). In a similar way, social scientists have been arguing for the inclusion of issues like the social and political feasibility of conservation schemes (Wilshusen et al. 2002: 17). However, too much effort has gone into the application of standardized criteria to different socioeconomic, geographic, and cultural settings, and insufficient attention has been paid to the fact that different problems should call for different types of solutions. The approach followed in this book is different. It first calls for the identification of the most relevant empirical factors affecting people's environmental behavior in each setting, focusing on the observation of actual practices, which should then be taken into account in the analysis and in shaping the type of conservation intervention adopted. In addition, every factor identified as influential on indigenous environmental behavior should be understood in the context of its interactions with other relevant factors. Likewise, factors belonging to different moments in time should be placed at different levels on a temporal scale.

In the case of the Wachiperi, some of the most relevant factors identified as influential in the intensity of their hunting practices are changes in settlement patterns, deep social disruptions created by massive deaths among the population and resettlement, changes in social roles according to gender, changes in food consumption patterns, reduced influence of spiritual beliefs, loss of hunting knowledge, diversification of livelihoods in the context of a mixed economy, and habitat degradation created as a result of immigration and the expansion of settlers' agricultural activities. From this list of influential aspects, livelihood diversification has been one of the most directly influential factors on hunting intensity. Its relevance has been recurrent across the examination of the historical processes in Chapter One, the changes of social roles according to gender in Chapter Two, and the analysis of contemporary factors in the present chapter.

Similarly, in the surveys and interviews I conducted, the question of why people of Queros hunt less now than in the past has consistently shown a pattern where nowadays they have other activities to attend to. Reduced availability of time to go hunting was reported as the main reason for their decreased hunting intensity. Interviewees also addressed the question of why people in Queros no longer go hunting on a frequent basis with answers like "perhaps because there is not enough time," "mostly when there is agricultural work to do," or "because of work, of course." The existence of other socioeconomic alternatives and the growing economic needs of the population were also reported as influential factors, illustrating the fact that the diversification of their livelihoods has been a key factor in shaping hunting intensity.

Ecosystem changes were also influential in this process. Shortly after the establishment of closer relationships with members of Western society, the hunting practices of the Wachiperi decreased as a result of temporary game scarcity in the forests near their community, which was promoted by changes in their settlement patterns and the increased presence of settlers. The concentration of the Wachiperi in a Baptist mission and the introduction of shotguns led to animal scarcity, which created a need to explore other, more efficient means of sustenance, such as fishing and agriculture. However, greater emphasis on fishing and agriculture contributed to a reduction in the practice of hunting, illustrating the influence of livelihood alternatives. Later, habitat disturbances created by settlers reduced even further the presence of forest animals in the area, since settlers cleared large parts of the forest for agricultural fields.

In a similar way, Chapter Two explored how changes in the food consumption patterns of the Wachiperi, especially toward products purchased in the market, have produced a greater need to invest more of their time and effort in income-generating activities. These activities include logging and trading, as well as sustainable enterprises like tourism and community-based conservation, which will be discussed in the next chapter. Agriculture is another activity that has become increasingly attractive for the people of Queros, since crops can be used for both subsistence and the market, providing them with the means to both acquire their new preferred types of food and combine them with traditional foods. Accordingly, hunting has been increasingly displaced from the privileged position it occupied several decades ago, when it was a main area of concern. This change is part of a repositioning trend directly associated to the diversification of their livelihoods, which is a process created by the transition of the Wachiperi from a subsistence economy toward a mixed economy. Market engagements promoted new behavioral patterns as part of their adaptation to the changing socioeconomic conditions.

Changes in gender roles also influenced the intensity of hunting among the Wachiperi. The current social expectations allow greater flexibility for both men and women to fulfill their gender roles. In the case of men, the customary requirement of bringing meat of forest animals to their households has expanded to include a greater variety in the type and source of the food, as long as the role as providers for their household is maintained. In the case of women, their role in persuading men to go hunting has switched to encouraging them to bring home food, especially market products, which are currently located at the top of their list of dietary preferences. Thus food expectations have influenced the decisions of the Wachiperi to focus on income-generating activities, while hunting has increasingly become a complementary endeavor.

The growing needs and desires of the people of Queros are consistent with their increasing engagement in market exchanges and the emergence of new productive activities as alternatives that nowadays the Wachiperi prefer over hunting. These changes reflect the fact that livelihood diversification has been one of the most directly influential factors shaping the intensity of Wachiperi hunting practices. The influence of livelihood diversification is explored in the next chapter.

Chapter IV

Diversification of Livelihoods

During my ethnographic work in Queros, people from the community sometimes uttered phrases that opened new lines of thought for exploration, with implications for my understanding of the social and environmental dynamics of the community. One of these phrases was expressed by a member of the community who works as a ranger and who said, "I used to hunt before, now I'm a conservationist." In this context, being a conservationist refers to his current situation, the role he assumed through his employment but not necessarily part of an immutable behavior. This phrase illustrates how the emergence of community-based conservation as a new socioeconomic activity has direct implications on the environmental behavior of the Wachiperi, especially due to the introduction of a new socioeconomic activity that has been affecting their lives in a significant way.

This chapter addresses the influence of livelihood diversification on the levels of hunting intensity among the Wachiperi, particularly in the last decade. The first section examines the recent orientation of the community toward commercial activities like agriculture and logging. The second section focuses on the emergence of sustainable enterprises, including community-based tourism and environmental conservation. The chapter ends with a discussion of the current expectations of the Wachiperi about improvements in their living conditions in terms of conservation as development.

101

The focus on livelihood diversification is a reflection of the growing orientation of the Wachiperi toward both subsistence and income-generating activities, which is consistent with the contemporary requirements of their mixed economy. The strategy adopted by the Wachiperi to achieve their goals is based on a combination of both traditional practices and market-oriented activities, which provide them with the necessary resources to satisfy their current needs and desires. Accordingly, activities that address these two purposes of agriculture and community-based conservation have acquired greater predominance among the Wachiperi. Contrastingly, subsistence-only activities like hunting and gathering have become less relevant in Wachiperi society. The current allocation of their limited time toward both subsistence and income-generating activities has been driving the attention of the Wachiperi away from subsistence-only practices. In other words, the Wachiperi today have a wider portfolio of activities that requires them to invest the limited productive resources available according to the degree of contribution toward the current satisfaction of their needs and desires, which is mostly achieved by activities that provide them with both subsistence and income benefits.

Commercial Activities

This section describes the current practices of commercial agriculture, logging, and local trade being conducted by the Wachiperi. They include the activities of people living in both Queros and Pillcopata in the last decade.

Agricultural Production

The main economic activity among the Wachiperi today is agriculture, which is conducted both for subsistence and commercial purposes. Improvements in the road conditions connecting the community of Queros with a point close to

Pillcopata made it possible for the Wachiperi to allocate part of their agricultural production toward the market, especially crops like cassava and rice. Their agricultural products are transported in small trucks. Instead of selling small amounts of agricultural products on a recurrent basis, they now sell larger harvests less often, adopting a commercial style that takes advantage of the new means of available transportation.

The levels of agricultural production in Queros have shown relative growth in the last few years. In 2008, the cultivated agricultural area increased by approximately 20%. However, in 2009, agricultural expansion was limited by their limited time for cultivation, since many men from Queros were hired as paid conservation rangers, an activity that demands a considerable amount of their time. Men are still responsible for establishing the agricultural plots, so their new employment situation has affected these activities. While some of the rangers were able to get time off to take care of their agricultural duties, the amount of work they could do in that limited period was significantly less than when they had full-time availability.

The main agricultural crops intended for the market are cassava and coca leaves. Other important crops are corn and beans. Rice is becoming another key product, since most of the new plots have been producing rice. However, it is important to note that while agricultural fields may have a predominant crop, oftentimes they also include additional sections with other types of crops intended for self-consumption. In addition, part of the agricultural production in Queros is used for the market and part for self-consumption, especially in the case of cassava. This distribution varies for each family, since each family cultivates and harvests different amounts.

The most profitable agricultural product is coca leaves, which are sold in Pillcopata. On average, people sell coca leaves about four times a year. However, most people in Queros grow coca leaves in smaller amounts and only for self-consumption. The next most profitable crop is rice. The volume of rice produced varies, but people who cultivate rice have sold around 1.2 tons on average, once a year. The third most profitable crop is cassava, which is the most common crop cultivated in Queros. People who cultivate cassava with a commercial orientation sell about 2.1 tons yearly, but there is considerable variation in the production according to the size of the areas cultivated for the market.

Most people in Queros cultivate more than one product simultaneously because risk diversification is perceived as important for them. As a result, income from agricultural activities is often a combination of multiple crops. This strategy is a form of diversifying their production, since market prices sometimes drop from one harvest season to the next, and also because of the risks posed by agricultural pests. Crops are often cultivated in different plots, because the uneven terrain creates the need to open them in different places. Where large patches of land exist, several crops can be cultivated in the same plot, establishing different sections for each crop.

Women in the community visit the agricultural fields to harvest small amounts of food almost on a daily basis. When men go to the fields, which they do less often than women, their main purpose is clearing the area around the crops from weeds and vines, thereby making sure there are no threats to their crops. Men are also the ones who apply insecticides and herbicides. This was first done by employing the roots of a plant (barbasco) to keep insects at bay, but since this root is increasingly scarce in the community, they now use chemical products bought in Pillcopata.

The increase in agricultural production with a commercial orientation has affected the hunting practices of the Wachiperi in direct ways. The most significant one is by diverting attention from hunting toward agriculture. The multiple tasks required in the agricultural cycle keep people busy, with limited time for subsistence-only activities. Thus a common pattern has emerged, which is characterized by greater allocation of time to activities that provide them with both subsistence and commercial products, like agriculture. In addition, the heaviest part of the agricultural work takes place during the dry season, when the opening of new agricultural plots takes place. The dry season is also the time when game is more available in the forest, as described in the subsection on ecological features in the previous chapter. Accordingly, the fact that these two activities demand people's attention at the same time has created the need to prioritize one of them, and they have favored agriculture over hunting.

Logging Practices

Commercial logging has become another important activity among the Wachiperi, especially in the last two decades. Initially they focused on harvesting fine woods like cedar (*Cedrela odorata*) and tornillo (*Cedrelinga catenaeformis*). Cutting cedar trees for sale is now forbidden by the government, and the Wachiperi have been enforcing that regulation. If a member of the community were to cut cedar trees, the agreement is that half of the cedar wood harvested would be taken over by the community as a form of punishment to prevent further misbehavior. However, fine woods have almost run out in the area during the last decade, with the exception of tornillo. As a result, timber harvesting is now focused on "less valuable" species. The category of less valuable timber includes a wide range of trees like the ones regionally known as pashaco, matapalo, caobilla, ojé, azucar huayo, alcanfor, and catahua, among others.

The main instrument for cutting wood used by the Wachiperi is the chain saw. Once the trees are cut down, they are sliced into smaller blocks on the spot and then transported to Pillcopata by land. Small trucks are used for transportation. The timber is sold to a few buyers in Pillcopata, who set a standard price according to the type of wood, and then ship it to the city of Cusco using larger trucks.

The logging cycle starts when a person identifies the trees to be cut down and estimates the amount of wood they can produce, so they can plan their harvesting activities based on that information. Afterwards, the trees are cut down and sliced into rectangular blocks, facilitating their transportation without any special equipment. Most of the logging is conducted by men, but women also participate through the establishment of logging camps. When men and their wives go to work for periods of up to two weeks at a time, they stay until the work is completed and the timber is ready for transport. In these cases, women play an important role in areas like transporting food, tools, and other goods, setting up and tending to the camp, cooking, gathering food, carrying water, and providing company for their husbands. Some women also participate in the commercialization of timber, even if they do not do the harvesting work themselves.

In the last few years it has become increasingly common for people from Queros to hire chain saw operators from outside the community to cut down their trees, up to the amount allowed by the community assembly to its members. Hiring chain saw operators started when the people from Queros harvesting timber did not possess the time, equipment, or strength to cut the trees themselves. This was also the case of some women in the community, who hired men to do the timber harvesting for them. Operators were hired on a temporary basis and paid based on the amount of wood they cut. Later on, the practice of hiring chain saw operators became more common because hired operators worked faster and required less effort by the person in charge, while the margin of profit was similar to the one they would have gotten had they done the work themselves.

Most of the timber in the Kosñipata Valley is harvested using legal permits of extraction granted by the government, but the trees are not always harvested from these authorized lands. As a result, the inhabitants of Queros have discovered in the past that people from surrounding areas have been harvesting wood from places inside their community territory. In these cases, they have to denounce the infraction to the police post in Pillcopata to immobilize the wood until the issue has been clarified, and then transfer the wood to the community. However, this process does not work well, because people from the community have to prove that the timber has been harvested from their community lands, which requires close surveillance and clear evidence. In addition, the information has to be accurate. On one occasion, people from Queros reported that a truckload of tornillo wood had been harvested from inside their community lands. However, the police inspection determined that the wood was not tornillo but other, less valuable wood. As a result, the police dismissed their claim and the wood was released to the person who harvested it. The place of extraction did not matter in this case. According to the widespread perception of the Wachiperi, the performance of the police regarding the control of illegal timber harvesting in the Kosñipata Valley is very inefficient.

The recent engagement of people from Queros in community-based conservation has seen a reduction in the levels of logging among the population. According to internal regulations agreed to by the community assembly, the maximum limits of timber harvesting for active members is three thousand square feet of tornillo wood and ten thousand square feet of less valuable wood per year. The limit of three thousand square feet of tornillo wood is recent; until 2008 it was five thousand square feet. Some people within the community do not completely agree with this reduction, but the pressure of the rest of the group has made them understand the need to become less dependent on profits from timber. As a means of control, the community chief now asks people to declare their intention to harvest wood and their estimated amounts at the beginning of the logging season. The chief then authorizes people from Queros to harvest according to community regulations, monitoring this activity and encouraging people to reduce their harvesting volumes.

The logging restrictions adopted by the community of Queros generated some internal political tensions. People who conducted most of the logging operations were not satisfied with the increased restrictions adopted by the community assembly. These differences were dealt with in community meetings, where people who disagreed openly voiced their opinions. The other community members listened and evaluated these claims, but they repeatedly ratified their desire to continue with the restrictions they had previous agreed to by majority vote, even if not everyone was satisfied. However, the expectation of the leaders is that people will eventually recognize the benefits of sustainable activities like tourism and conservation and join the rest of the community members who are already supporting this new course of action.

Logging activities have had a direct effect on the intensity of hunting practices among the Wachiperi. As in the case of commercial agriculture, logging demands greater investment of time and effort during the dry season, which is also when game is more readily available. The dry season is especially important because temporary logging roads are constructed along the dry parts of the rivers, which flood during the rainy season. This situation has created the need to choose one activity over the other, and people from Queros have for the most part chosen logging over hunting. The profitability of logging is a more attractive incentive than the meat provided by hunting, since people's perceived expectations for the improvement of their living conditions increasingly include activities that provide people with monetary income, characteristic of their current mixed economy. As a result, greater attention to logging has been diverting attention from hunting and other subsistence-only activities in general. Moreover, the fact that hunting is not seen as a source of cash even though income is important in the current mixed economy of the Wachiperi is an important dimension of their environmental behavior that reflects the complexity of the different factors at play.

Other Commercial Activities

Agriculture and logging are activities conducted mainly by people living in Queros on a full-time basis. In the case of people from Queros living in Pillcopata, commercial activities also include local trade. One of the most economically prosperous persons from Queros is the owner of a small store in Pillcopata that sells grocery items and provides services such as a public telephone, bus tickets from Pillcopata to Cusco, money transfers, and other services that leave the owner with a percentage of the sales. A section of the business administered by this merchant's son also includes renting computers with access to the Internet, charging customers based on an hourly fee. This store is also a place where people from Queros meet and socialize during their visits to Pillcopata.

Other people from Queros living in Pillcopata who also conduct trading activities include a woman from Queros who sells a warm beverage made of quinoa in the market of Pillcopata, where local residents come regularly to buy it for breakfast. This business takes place in the early hours of the morning. Likewise, a woman whose husband has a full-time job as a school teacher in Pillcopata installed a small booth for selling carbonated drinks in her living room, where neighbors can buy them instead of walking to the stores that are farther away. In addition, this woman prepares natural drinks and popsicles made out of forest products like aguaje, which are regularly consumed by Pillcopata residents on warm days.

Trading activities have also diverted the attention of people from hunting. Their engagement in commercial behavior has created a greater need for them to remain in Pillcopata, since the services they provide have created a regular flow of customers who would be disappointed if the owners stopped providing that service. Their need to maintain a good relationship with their customers has encouraged those involved in trading to remain in town most of the time so their customers do not start shopping at other stores.

Sustainable Enterprises

This section describes the environmentally sustainable, income-generating activities that have been adopted by the Wachiperi in recent years, including community-based tourism and environmental conservation. These activities are consistent with the principles of "defense of the ecological equilibrium, the preservation and the rational use of natural resources" in their community territory, as stipulated in the internal statute of the community (Queros 1996: 6).

Community-Based Tourism

For the past fifteen years, people from Queros have been trying to develop a community-based tourism program. Inspired by the regular flow of tourists stopping in the town of Pillcopata on their way to visit Manu National Park, people of Queros figured that tourists might also be persuaded to visit the preserved forests surrounding their community and decided to organize their own tourism program. One of their goals has been to promote the training of community members as tour guides and ecological interpreters so that the community can manage their own tourism program.

With the idea of tourism in mind, they tried to obtain the institutional support of different organizations working in the area. In 2000 they started working together with the Pro-Manu Project. This project supported the development of an environmental management plan for the community, which included ecotourism as a core activity. The planning process documented a series of tourist attractions within the community territory, organizing them in three tourist circuits that ranged from one to three days in length. These circuits included visits to the community of Queros, the Hinkiori petroglyphs described in Chapter One, and the Entoro and Rio Blanco Rivers. These places would allow visitors to see animals in the forest, in the rivers, and at their saltlicks. Animals more likely to be seen by visitors included peccaries, tapirs, deer, monkeys, butterflies, fish, frogs, giant trees, and a variety of birds, especially macaws, parrots, toucans, wild turkeys, doves, and falcons, among others (Pinasco 2002: 63–64).

Budget limitations and abandonment of the project by the person in charge of supporting this initiative prevented the implementation of this environmental management plan.

While partial progress was made in areas like opening trails for visitors and acquiring camping equipment for them, the lack of permanent institutional support stalled these activities. Further attempts of the community to move forward with their ecotourism initiative were limited by the lack of marketing mechanisms to attract visitors, especially environmentally conscious people who were also fit to conduct long walks in the forest. This became a significant challenge, especially considering that organizing a tourism program was a brand-new experience for the people of Queros.

The lack of progress in the area of ecotourism created a need for the community to reevaluate their strategy. Accordingly, around 2006 the community decided to switch the direction of their efforts toward cultural tourism. Instead of showing visitors the biological attractions of the area, they decided to share their community way of life. In this new scheme, visitors were introduced to the history of the Wachiperi and their struggles for the acquisition of land, their expectations for the recovery of their ancestral cultural values, and the current engagement of the community in conservation. Visitors were also shown the ancestral dances of the Wachiperi, where performers wore traditional robes. Community members also organized arrow shooting contests for tourists, taught them how to make baskets, and offered them some of the food and drinks of the Wachiperi, like cassava, masato, palm core cooked in a piece of bamboo, fish, and the meat of forest animals, among others. At night, visitors were invited to sit around a campfire, where members of the community, including men and women, told stories about the mythical origins of the Wachiperi and sang ancestral songs about their interactions with forest animals. The return of the visitors to Pillcopata was organized in rafts along the Queros River, making a stop to see the Hinkiori petroglyphs.

These activities were planned by the community members themselves. Some of the details built on ideas previously developed for their ecotourism plan, and they also incorporated suggestions from friends and allies outside the community to improve their planning details. They also focused more on the marketing part of their tourist circuit. The development of a community website by a member of the community played an important role in providing information to potential visitors, and the use of electronic mail also favored the establishment of distant communications. The leaders of the community also started coordinating with some regional organizations working in the area of tourism, which brought groups of visitors to the community, generating some income for the population. In 2008, the community of Queros received two groups of foreign tourists, and in the first half of 2009 they received three groups of tourists from Italy, England, and Spain. Each group had six people on average and stayed for three days and two nights in the community. In 2009, Queros received a total of eight groups of tourists, which is four times higher than the number of groups they received in 2008, indicating a growing trend of this activity.

Tourism-related activities in Queros were led by Walter Quertehuari, a community member who was appointed as tourism coordinator by the group. The tourism coordinator negotiates costs with the guides of the tour groups or the organizations that bring them, prepares budget tables, and reports to the community on a regular basis. His role communicating with tour guides and external organizations was favored by his access to e-mail and instant messaging, since he runs a small business in Pillcopata renting computers with access to the Internet. The cost of the services people from Queros provide for tourists were decided in a community assembly, as were the updates to these prices when they were required.

The current manner in which tourism operations are conducted, which was agreed to by the community, is that every individual that provides a service for tourists gets paid for those services. People are selected on a rotational basis to make sure every person participates. People who transport tourists on a raft, for instance, get paid a set amount according to the number of people transported.

Cooking is an activity where each adult woman in the community assumes responsibility for feeding the group of tourists for one day and gets paid an established amount multiplied by the number of meals and the number of tourists. The main women in each household take charge of organizing the cooking for that day, and often they are expected to include the meat of forest animals to provide tourists with an "authentic" culinary experience. So it is up to women to ask men in their families to go hunting for this purpose. Sometimes they ask a man from the community who is not a relative to hunt, and they negotiate the compensation directly. However, women decide if they want to include meat or not, since they are the ones who determine the type of food to be served and which non-meat products are also acceptable, like palm cores, plantains, and forest fruits. Thus women do not always depend on men to acquire food products. From this perspective, the way tourism is being conducted in Queros has an empowering potential for women, since women's contributions have acquired a higher value within this market system.

While women's labor in Queros is experiencing a process of commodification, at the same time it is providing them with economic benefits and a potentially higher status in society. However, tourism activities in the community are in an early stage and their full implications still remain to be defined. What is becoming increasingly clear is that the joint efforts of men and women are bringing good results for this community project, since men would not be able to do it by themselves with similar levels of success. A collaborative work style based on an equitable distribution of benefits regardless of gender is allowing the Wachiperi to make significant progress toward their community goals. These include higher levels of income while protecting their forests and strengthening parts of their traditional culture that are currently at risk of disappearance, in addition to higher levels of general satisfaction, a stronger sense of cultural identity, pride, and optimism about their future as an indigenous community.

Getting organized for tourism was one of the main challenges for people in the community, but after the initial visits of tourists, people started to feel more comfortable with the idea of hosting them. As the tourism coordinator of the community stated, "At the beginning people used to say 'I don't know,' 'I am not going to cook because I do not know how to cook for gringos,' but people are responding better now...the idea was to start doing activities and learn in the process." The visit of each group of tourists represents a learning opportunity for the people from Queros, since those in the community usually reflect together on their strengths and shortcomings after each visit, making plans for improving the quality of their service for subsequent tourist visits.

In relation to their environmental behavior, the original community initiative toward ecotourism discouraged continuous hunting, at least at some saltlicks and parts of the forest where their habitat was less disturbed, since animals were expected to be left alone and become an attraction for visitors. Hunting was still considered appropriate in other parts of the community territory, closer to the community or in areas of the forest already disturbed. However, because of the greater concentration of animals in the areas reserved for ecotourism, the chances of finding animals in the disrupted areas of the forest were smaller, reducing their return rates and discouraging hunting. The change in the focus of the Wachiperi toward cultural tourism did not affect this situation, since the perception of forest animals as a valuable resource for tourism is still present.

In contemporary Wachiperi perceptions, forest animals are increasingly seen as a resource that should be saved for special occasions, like the visits of tourists, when the community could provide the visitors with a local eating experience. Accordingly, the inhabitants of Queros have been for the most part reducing the hunting pressure on the saltlicks and the less disturbed areas of the forest. These places are still a valid alternative to hunt for special events when it is necessary to obtain meat, especially in cases when people are unable to hunt animals in areas closer to the village.

    In synthesis, the orientation of the activities undertaken by the community of Queros toward tourism has been influencing the intensity of their hunting practices in significant ways, decreasing the frequency of their hunting trips and discouraging regular hunting in less-disturbed places where forest animals dwell, since forest animals are now perceived as an important resource in their community-based tourism program. This perception is the reason why the Wachiperi have agreed not to share the knowledge about the location of saltlicks with settlers to avoid the risk that the hunting activities of settlers could have on the availability of game.

Environmental Conservation

    In July 2008, the community of Queros obtained the rights to administer an area of 6,975 hectares of tropical rain forest, which is approximately 27 square miles of land located next to their community territory. They named it "Reserva Ecológica Haramba Queros Wachiperi," which is addressed here as the conservation concession. The Peruvian government granted this permit to the community of Queros for the conservation of the biodiversity inside the area, for a renewable period of forty years. This event marked the beginning of a novel process for both the community and the government, since this was the first conservation concession granted to an indigenous community in Peru. During the signing of the agreement, the director of the government agency in charge of protected areas optimistically stated that the Peruvian government intends to continue granting concessions to indigenous communities, because they are the ones who know their territory and are consequently the best suited to protect their ancestral lands (Inrena 2008). This attitude by the government is consistent with an emerging trend in Peru to incorporate indigenous communities in the management of protected areas for conservation.

The involvement of the community of Queros in this conservation concession involved several steps. It started when members of the community were informed that an investor from Pillcopata had submitted an application to the Peruvian government for an ecotourism concession in the forests next to their community lands. This situation triggered a reaction among people from Queros, who consider the lands surrounding their community to be part of their ancestral territory. The possibility of an external person acquiring access rights to those lands unified the population around this common theme, strengthening their sense of territorial and cultural identity. They started negotiations with the investor who presented the claim, and they agreed to split the requested area in two. The investor modified his application and then requested only half of the original territory considered, leaving the other half available. Thus people from Queros were able to submit their own application to gain access to the other half.

The first option considered by people from Queros was to request an expansion of their territory to include the lands next to the community. However, this territorial expansion strategy was quickly discarded, since this approach had been tried unsuccessfully for at least ten years. Their lack of success was in part due to the small number of inhabitants, which is around sixty, including some people that are part of the community but no longer live physically in Queros. Accordingly, they decided it was time to adopt a new strategy.

Their second alternative to gain access to the lands next to their community was to request a concession for ecotourism from the government. This idea was consistent with their former interest in ecotourism, as described in the previous subsection. However, one of the main problems with ecotourism concessions was that administrators were required to pay an annual fee to the government as a means of monetary retribution for the income-generating use of the area, involving annual payments of more than a thousand dollars after the fifth year. Since the community had limited access to monetary resources and the potential revenues from tourism were uncertain, an ecotourism concession was not considered to be feasible at the time.

The third option considered by people from Queros, which was especially promoted by college-educated young members of the community, was to obtain a territorial concession for biodiversity conservation. Central in shaping the direction of this process was the role of Walter Quertehuari, who has a college degree in education with a concentration in natural sciences and ecology. Quertehuari had also worked as an officer for the Indigenous Federation of the Madre de Dios River and its Tributaries, where he was exposed to urban social dynamics, institutional procedures of nonprofits, and external discourses about indigenous peoples and the environment, which allowed him to envision new alternatives after returning to his community. People from Queros had also worked in coordination with mainstream conservation organizations in the past, so they were familiar with the idea of implementing projects to protect the environment.

The interest of the community in a conservation concession to access the area they considered part of their ancestral territory captured the attention of the Asociación para la Conservación de la Cuenca Amazónica (ACCA). Since 2004, this organization had been looking to expand their operations in the area. The initial interest of the ACCA was to support sustainable development efforts of local communities, including ecotourism, by employing a micro-finance scheme. However, after the community approached the ACCA, both parties agreed that the best strategy to address their mutual goals was to request a conservation concession. As a result, the ACCA and the community of Queros signed a cooperation agreement, a partnership in which the ACCA would provide institutional, financial, and technical support to the community of Queros for the management of their concession.

With the support of the ACCA, the Wachiperi were successful in their application for a conservation concession. After the government granted this concession, the community appointed Walter Quertehuari as the chief of the concession, and shortly after they selected a group of five rangers from the community, with salaries initially provided by the ACCA. In the first year after the concession was granted, these rangers conducted surveillance of activities in the concession, while the concession chief led the preparation of their strategic management plan and a training plan for concession rangers, among other activities.

The engagement of the community of Queros in this conservation concession had a considerable influence on their hunting practices. The most direct effect was that people hired as concession rangers had less available time to hunt, since their activities in the concession demand a considerable amount of their time. Their decreased availability of time also reduced their involvement in commercial agriculture and logging activities. In addition, the idea of conserving the forests and their biological resources strengthened the belief that hunting should not be conducted in areas near the concession to conserve its animal populations. This attitude is associated with the community goal of constructing a research center in the future where researchers can study the biological processes within the conservation concession, as described in their concession management plan. This research center will be located within the lands of the community, next to the border of the concession.

The abundance of forest animals in the area is expected to contribute to the attractiveness of the research center, which in turn is expected to become a source of additional income for the community, since researchers are expected to pay fees to the community during their stay. The potential economic benefits have been a source of motivation to conserve the forests and their animal inhabitants.[8] In synthesis, the recent engagement of the community of Queros in the conservation of the biological resources within and near its conservation

---

[8] This situation does not support the idea of "discount rate" proposed by some scholars (Alvard 1995: 802; Kirby et al. 2002: 292). The recent experience of the Wachiperi indicates that they are restraining from benefiting from hunting in the present to obtain greater benefits of a different kind in the future.

concession has contributed to a decrease in the intensity of their hunting practices in a significant way.

Expectations for Development

The Wachiperi are no longer an indigenous group concerned only with subsistence. Their contemporary way of life includes a wide variety of needs that require them to pursue income-generating activities, defining the current orientation of the productive activities in the community of Queros as a mixed economy. In addition to subsistence, the current goals of people in Queros include sending their children to college, accessing different types of technology, improving their means of transportation, increasing food security, protecting their ancestral territory, and conserving the local forests. To achieve these goals, they have launched different strategies like commercial agriculture and logging. They have also adopted sustainable enterprises like tourism and environmental conservation, which have been increasingly accepted by the Wachiperi. The orientation of the community toward environmental conservation and tourism has even begun displacing unsustainable activities like logging.

This process presents certain elements of what Igoe and Fortwangler call "market-driven conservation" (2007: 1), based on a mercantilist logic underlying the relationships between the multiple agents involved in conservation within the current neoliberal formation. However, it is important to recognize that market-oriented processes among the Wachiperi coexist with subsistence activities, and neoliberal ideas coexist with non-neoliberal elements of the indigenous culture. These two dimensions provide a complex local landscape that should not be eclipsed by the analysis of larger market processes. The idea of a mixed configuration that includes traditional and neoliberal elements provides a more accurate depiction of the current situation of the Wachiperi.

At a more practical level, the emerging trend toward sustainable activities in Queros reflects the current strategy adopted by the Wachiperi toward conservation as development. The conservation of forests within and outside their community is not only an end in itself, but also a means to improve their life conditions in the long term. In the ancestral Wachiperi perception, the forest was a source of life, since it provided its inhabitants with all the resources they needed for their subsistence. While considerable changes have occurred since they established a permanent relationship with Western society, the local forests are still important in people's perceptions, linking people of the community with their history and ancestry and contributing to the strengthening of their sense of cultural identity. As the leader of Queros pointed out, their idea is "to move forward with our culture, integrating our culture with our ancient transcendence."

Conserving the local forests is also a way for people of Queros to maintain a community space where they can conduct their lives and plan their future in a less disruptive way than in previous decades, providing them with a geographical point of reference and a platform of stability in a constantly changing world. When the horizon is unclear, as is often the case with the recent endeavors assumed by the Wachiperi, the village of Queros and its surrounding forests and animals provide a sense of place that allows them to organize their space and maintain a sense of historical continuity.

In terms of the potential to fulfill the development expectations of people in the community, community-based conservation has been increasingly acknowledged as a valid means to achieve their collective goals. This has been especially evident in direct effects like the salaries paid to the five concession rangers and the concession chief. The main job of these rangers so far has been the monitoring and surveillance of threats to biodiversity within the concession area. Another benefit of conserving forest animals is to make them available for tourists, since tourism is increasingly becoming a relevant source of income for the population of Queros. Accordingly, animals need to be saved as a resource for tourism, discouraging regular hunting near the concession. Likewise, the potential income from researchers' fees if a biological research center is implemented is also a significant incentive for people to conserve biodiversity.

The adoption of different socioeconomic activities also represents a strategy to diversify their production as a precaution adopted in relation to the changing character of regional socioeconomic processes. As people from Queros reported, they try not to rely on only one source of income, since outcomes are oftentimes uncertain, especially in the case of agricultural production, where harvests and prices may vary significantly from one year to the next. As a result, having multiple sources of income has increasingly become a more attractive option than concentrating on only one activity.

In relation to their hunting practices, the recent engagement of the Wachiperi in income-generating activities has driven attention away from hunting, since activities like commercial agriculture and logging absorb most of their time and energy. The emergence of sustainable enterprises has also had a direct effect on reducing the practice of subsistence hunting. In the case of tourism, the need to have forest animals available when tourists come has encouraged the adoption of an attitude that perceives forest animals as renewable stock to be used in a sustainable way to avoid scarcity. This view is strongest among community leaders, but it is spreading among the population of Queros in general.

The need to maintain local biodiversity is also related to the possibility of successfully implementing a biological research center. Thus people have been avoiding activities that could potentially affect the availability of animals within and near their conservation concession. These activities have been encouraging people to reduce the practice of hunting. In addition, when people from Queros do hunt, they conduct this activity with a cautionary attitude to avoid affecting the availability of forest animals, preferably in areas of the forest already disturbed. This conservationist stance is part of their growing realization that forest resources are limited. As a man from the community of Queros pointed out, "Before we used to think that biodiversity is unlimited, but now we realize that it can be exterminated."

The Wachiperi attitudes toward the environment, grounded in their ancestral and current perceptions of the forest, favored the establishment of a partnership between the community of Queros and an environmental organization. They planned and conducted activities based on their overlapping expectations. This partnership produced results like their conservation concession. The fact that the Wachiperi approached this organization in the first place reflects the larger socioeconomic and cultural changes experienced by the Wachiperi in recent decades. These changes have deep implications for their current way of life, especially in terms of the diversification of their livelihoods. While partnerships between indigenous communities and environmental organizations are immersed in unequal relations of power unfavorable to indigenous groups (Igoe 2005: 378; Chernela 2005: 630), these relationships also represent the opportunity for indigenous communities to develop greater capacity for community-based conservation. Greater familiarity with the Western work style, based on written documents like project proposals, management plans, progress reports, and itemized budgets, has the potential to provide the Wachiperi with a better negotiating position as time passes and they develop new skills to use in support of their own initiatives. This situation is illustrated by the process of "cooption from below" (Mosse 2005: 239), which is further described in the next chapter, along with the effects of cultural change and interactions with outsiders.

Chapter V

Hunting in a Changing Society

On several occasions when I mentioned that I was studying the hunting practices of an indigenous group in the Peruvian rain forest, I heard a number of questions based on troubling assumptions. People unfamiliar with the current reality of indigenous groups asked me questions like "do they still live like primitives?" or "do they shrink the heads of their enemies?" or "do they eat human flesh?" The recurrence of these questions suggests that widespread misconceptions influence these thoughts. Part of the reason is due to media representations, which oftentimes portray the more "exotic" dimensions of the indigenous way of life. A recent article published in a Peruvian newspaper refers to indigenous peoples of the rain forest as "ignorant, primitive, and ferocious Indians from the pre-agricultural age," while also describing them as "paleolithic" and "savages wearing loincloths."[9] Even many anthropologists still equate indigenous groups that practice hunting with hunting-gathering societies, which are significantly different. These comments and questions reflect a disconcerting lack of knowledge about the contemporary way of life of indigenous groups in tropical rain forests, and in many cases also reflect an underlying ethnic discrimination.

This book attempts to contribute to a more accurate understanding of the current living conditions of indigenous

---

[9] This article, written by a columnist of the Peruvian newspaper *Correo* (Bedoya 2009), was deemed the most racist article of that year by UK-based nonprofit organization Survival International.

groups. This chapter describes the most relevant contemporary processes in Wachiperi society and analyzes their influence on the current hunting practices of people in Queros. The process of cultural change that has taken place in the last few decades among the Wachiperi is addressed first, followed by a discussion of the greater interactions between the Wachiperi and outsiders in the last decade. The examination of these processes complements the previous chapter by illustrating how broader social dynamics have been shaping the current diversification of indigenous livelihoods, linking the specific factors affecting hunting intensity identified with other factors at a broader level of analysis. The chapter ends with a discussion about the need to incorporate these contemporary trends into our understanding of the current environmental behavior of indigenous groups living in tropical rain forests.

Cultural Change

In this section I address cultural change among the Wachiperi, including changes in their marriage practices and family relationships, the introduction of a new educational system, the greater generational divide among people from different age groups, and the presence of globalizing trends in the way of life of the community.

Marriage Practices

Changes in the marriage practices of the Wachiperi are an important indicator of larger transformations in their culture. Before the establishment of permanent relations with members of Western society, marriage ceremonies were public acts where the parents of the bride and groom legitimized the union. Parents had a strong say in the selection of the wedding partner of their daughters. As Lyon described it, "A man had to obtain permission of his future wife's parents in order to marry her. If the family was agreeable the ceremony took place. A girl had no veto power over her parents' choice" (Lyon 1967: 28). Marriage ceremonies were usually associated with fishing expeditions involving the families of the marrying couple, which provided food for the celebrations of this event, as well as a space for social interaction between members of the two families. Today, these public celebrations have disappeared. Marital unions are mainly conducted as an informal process where couples agree to live together. Talks are also held involving the parents, but mainly as a way of informing them of the decision made by the couple. Some people have gone through civil marriage according to Peruvian law, but these represent less than 14% of the total number of couples, according to a survey I conducted in Queros.

Family composition is another related change. In the middle of the twentieth century, the Wachiperi lived in large houses containing multiple nuclear families linked by kinship. Nowadays, one of the most visible changes is that houses are small and usually contain a single nuclear family. Elder members of the family live with one of their younger relatives. Single adult males oftentimes live with their relatives as well, but mainly on a temporary basis, since they are expected to build their own houses at some point. They can also change houses according to the status of their interactions with the family, usually selecting the household that treats them better. Single men sometimes make camps by their farms but usually sleep and eat within one of the households. The number of children per couple has also decreased in the last few decades, contributing toward a reduction in the average family size.

In the 1960s, the age for people to marry was about twenty-five (Lyon 1967: 28). Today, most people in the community of Queros form couples at different ages. There are two men in the community past the age of thirty-five who do not have a spouse yet. In the case of the youngest couple, they started living together when the woman was sixteen and the man twenty-five. The fact that some people start families at a younger age has been reported as one of the main reasons why conjugal separations are common these days. About one-third of the adults from Queros in a conjugal relationship have had a previous relationship, and in most cases they had children resulting from their prior relationships. The high rate of separations among couples has created new challenges in family relationships, since in many cases it is unclear what type of treatment half-siblings should be given. This uncertainty is especially common among children and teenagers, affecting the fluidity of their social interactions.

The rate of interethnic marriages has also increased significantly in the last two decades. According to the community census I conducted in 2008, approximately 92% of the conjugal unions of people from Queros younger than sixty-five are heterosexual unions between Wachiperi members of the community and people who came from other parts of the country. One of the main reasons was the custom of people marrying outside their households. As Lyon wrote, there was a "house exogamous" marriage tradition among the Wachiperi, who considered it appropriate to marry anyone except people considered as enemies and prohibited kin, which included parallel cousins (Lyon 1967: 29). Another reason was the low population density in Queros, which decreased people's chances of finding suitable partners within the community. There were cases where people from Queros married others from the same community but later separated, either by choice or death, and acquired new partners from a different ethnic group afterwards. These interethnic unions are present in similar proportion among men and women from Queros.

Most newcomers who later became members of Queros by establishing conjugal unions were originally Quechua-speaking people who came from the Andean region, in addition to people from the ethnic groups Matsiguenka, Amarakaeri, Aymara, and Spanish-speaking people from the region. This situation introduced new cultural values into the community, affecting social expectations and livelihoods. The most influential individuals were the ones from the Andean region, whose cultural values predisposed them to conduct production activities with a more clearly defined commercial orientation, such as agriculture and logging.

In relation to hunting, changes in their marriage practices have affected their patterns of meat distribution. The ancestral custom was to share the meat of hunted animals among the rest of the members of their large households, generating the need for people to give some meat in return, which created a continuous cycle of mutual debt. The decreasing size of the households turned families into more independent units, and therefore men were no longer required to go hunting in order to fulfill obligations of reciprocity. Accordingly, changes in marriage practices are also likely to have contributed to a reduction in the intensity of hunting among the Wachiperi.

Educational System

One of the most significant drivers of change in the Wachiperi culture was the introduction of an external educational system in the 1960s. As described by Pinasco, Baptist missionaries tried to teach the Wachiperi the principles of the Christian faith since 1961 and established the first school in 1968 (2002: 32). However, one of the main purposes seems to have been the conversion of the Wachiperi to Christianity, lecturing them about the Bible for about two hours each day, as well as teaching them reading and writing skills in Spanish. The school focused on the education of children and young people, but the preaching activities of the missionaries included the Wachiperi population as a whole. Since that time, the exposure of the Wachiperi to external ideas has been a continuous process that gradually introduced a new system of ideas, values, and perceptions associated with the Western knowledge brought by the school. Likewise, the school promoted the idea of education as a means of social mobility, where students could achieve higher living standards based on their educational accomplishments.

An elementary school where the community of Queros is currently located was first built in 1976, as a result of the collective work of the community (Pinasco 2002: 32). This building was improved in the 1990s with the financial support of Pro-Naturaleza, a national environmental nonprofit. The school functions with one classroom and one teacher only for all elementary grades. A renewal of the roof was conducted in 2008 with the support of the government, and in 2009 they renewed other parts with the support of the Asociación para la Conservación de la Cuenca Amazónica (ACCA).

In 2009, the school had nine students ranging from six to sixteen years old, distributed from first to sixth grade. Three of these students were children whose parents were not members of the community of Queros, but were invited to attend classes in Queros to reach the minimum number of students required for the school to remain open. The community of Queros developed an agreement with a couple living in an area neighboring their community territory, offering to provide food and shelter for their children so they could study in Queros on a full-time basis. This was a mutually beneficial agreement, since these children would have probably remained without access to education without this type of arrangement. In a similar way, the community developed an agreement with a family of former Andean immigrants. This family was asked to send its two children to the school in Queros, and in exchange, the family was able to use community lands to conduct their agricultural activities. Later on, individuals from this family were incorporated as community members.

Classes at the school are delivered in Spanish, since the teachers assigned to Queros mostly come from the Andean region. They are normally assigned to the school in Queros on a temporary basis, oftentimes changing teachers every year. Accordingly, teachers do not know much about the Wachiperi culture in general, delivering an education with standard content developed at the national level. As described by Pinedo, the intercultural training of the teachers and the educational curriculum being implemented at the elementary school in the community of Queros are not sufficient to make the school a place of reproduction of ancestral Wachiperi values and knowledge (2008: 17). Even though some teachers have made efforts to organize educational activities based on the Wachiperi culture, as in the case of customary dances and school assignments about ancestral myths, these efforts have not been conducted in a systematic way. Moreover, the context in which these activities have been organized has been deprived of the original context, purpose, and expectations that form the underlying purposes of educational activities.

One of the most significant changes introduced through the school is the utilitarian perspective of the forest and its animal inhabitants. In the national educational curricula, plants and animals are perceived as natural resources, with an intrinsic potential for providing concrete benefits. Forms of beneficial resources include both subsistence activities and the harvesting of natural products with a commercial orientation. While this exploitation is expected to be kept at levels that do not threaten their renewal capacity, the utilitarian perception of the utilization of plants and animals as a measure of their value is present as an underlying assumption in the different educational content. This new perception has also displaced the spiritual dimension of the forest inhabitants and the influence they exerted a few decades ago, as the indigenous views of the forest have been secularizing. This secularization removes key spiritual elements that were previously influential, like punishments associated with improper behavior in relation to forest animals. Accordingly, the social control provided by ancestral values and beliefs has been gradually displaced, and later attempts to fill this gap with programs to raise environmental awareness via the school have been mostly disconnected from the sociocultural reality of the Wachiperi.

The progressive loss of traditional knowledge has generated some level of resistance among community leaders and elders from Queros. One of the main ideas to stop this process has been to request the regional branch of the Ministry of Education to designate a school teacher in Queros trained in intercultural and bilingual education and who is familiar with Amazonian cultures and the rain forest environment. Another attempt to prevent the loss of the ancestral knowledge of the

Wachiperi is the strengthening of their cultural expressions via tourism initiatives, which have allowed them to pay closer attention to their traditional myths, songs, and ancestral techniques for making clothes, among other activities. These activities have raised awareness about the need to prevent further loss of traditional culture and to undertake activities that integrate their ancestral culture with their current expectations. The implementation of an ethno-development plan (cf. Andrade et al. 2006) was an attempt to create a program that would allow people from Queros to produce handicrafts and facilitate the transmission of knowledge from elders to the young, but this project did not prosper. The trend toward cultural loss is an issue of concern for people in Queros.

The adoption of new knowledge delivered by the school has also influenced people's hunting behavior in the community of Queros. The fact that the school tends to emphasize external knowledge over indigenous knowledge has defined a value system that excludes knowledge associated with traditional activities, such as that related to hunting animals. This effect is part of a system of unequal power relations, where Western knowledge is positioned as the dominant one, especially in a context of ethnic discrimination against indigenous groups of the rain forest. Instead of encouraging students to become proficient hunters, the school promoted the idea of becoming professionals, like a teacher or an agricultural engineer, able to acquire more specialized external knowledge to improve the living conditions of the population. Accordingly, the school has indirectly discouraged students from acquiring knowledge related to hunting activities or even pursuing subsistence hunting as a priority in their lives. Likewise, attendance at school requires a considerable investment of time and effort, leaving less time available to students for both learning how to hunt and conducting hunting activities, especially during the initial stages of learning. The school also defines a set of expectations of students' future livelihoods. In sum, the introduction of a new educational system has been influential in decreasing the intensity of hunting practices among the Wachiperi, mainly by introducing a new set of priorities in terms of knowledge that diverts attention from hunting, but also by reducing the time the students have available to conduct hunting activities.

Generational Divide

The process of cultural change experienced by the Wachiperi in the last decades has produced a considerable generational divide among the current population of Queros. The differences between age groups are pronounced, especially in terms of worldviews. These mainly refer to environmental knowledge, people's perceptions of the forest, including some degree of commodification of natural resources, as well as spiritual beliefs and moral values related to their environmental behavior that have been affected by increased consumption of manufactured products.

While age differences do not define clear patterns in terms of market-oriented practices like commercial agriculture and logging activities, their goals in life in some cases present considerable differences. The older generation is more likely to be content with having their basic needs fulfilled, but the younger generation has expectations that include greater secondary needs, which produces higher levels of consumption. An example is the case of transportation used to travel from Pillcopata to Queros. Young people from the community increasingly use motorcycles, even if they consume a considerable part of their income. For the most part, they hire the services of motorcycle owners from Pillcopata, but two people from Queros have recently acquired motorcycles.

Beyond transportation, the younger generation is also more concerned with the generation of monetary income than older people. Since in previous years logging was one of the most profitable activities conducted by people in the community, it is one of the young people's preferred activities. The volume of timber harvested by young people is higher than the one of older people. In the case of people hired as rangers of the conservation concession, their additional income has allowed them to increase their levels of spending. The consumption of manufactured products by the younger generation has also become more pronounced in the last decade. Examples include the substitution of reusable pieces of cloth for disposable diapers, canned food, noodles, increased consumption of bottled beer and cigarettes, especially during festivities, among other expenses related to their frequent visits to the town of Pillcopata.

While the levels of consumption of external products among the Wachiperi are significantly lower than those of settlers in the area, their growing exposure to available goods for purchase has generated new needs, desires, and consumption habits among the younger members of the community. Likewise, people who experienced life in the city have tended to lose their motivation to resume customary activities of subsistence like hunting practices after coming back to their community. As a young man from Queros stated, "When someone goes to live in the city for some time and then comes back, there is not the same enthusiasm to say 'I'm going hunting' like before."

The generational contrasts in Queros are mainly evident between the young and the elderly, since people between thirty and sixty years of age, who fall in the middle-age spectrum, constitute the majority of the people living in Queros. This group presents a high level of internal variability in their consumption patterns. Internal economic differentiation between members of the community of Queros is another relevant aspect, since some members of the community have greater income than others, especially those conducting commercial activities in the town of Pillcopata. Their trading activities for the most part keep them busy, preventing them from having enough time to go hunting, especially when their desire for the meat of forest animals can be satisfied by purchasing the meat of forest animals in Pillcopata. As a member from Queros pointed out, "These people do not go hunting, they do not want to go anymore, but they still eat the meat of animals hunted by others."

This generational and economic divide means that activities of subsistence like hunting have become less relevant for the younger generation and people involved in trading activities. While some of them still go hunting on certain occasions, they do so mostly by accepting invitations of their friends and relatives to join them in hunting parties. For them, hunting is mainly a complementary activity and no longer a significant means of subsistence.

There is also a recreational component to hunting, since conducting short walks in the forest after several days without leaving the area near the village can be a welcome activity. Nevertheless, the low frequency of hunting in general indicates that hunting occupies a low level of interest in the ranking of current priorities. As an elderly person from the community of Queros described it, "Civilization is upon us, it is not like before anymore. Now we know its benefits; that is why we do not want to go hunting but do other activities instead."

Globalizing Tendencies

Cultural change is influenced not only by local and regional interactions but increasingly by global processes as well. In the last two decades in particular, the Wachiperi experienced a number of processes that have also become common in other parts of the world. One of them is the "deterritorialization" of indigenous communities, characterized by a situation where ethnic groups "increasingly operate in ways that transcend specific territorial boundaries" (Appadurai 2003: 192). As described in Chapter Three, the community of Queros includes people living both inside and outside the community territory as a result of their recent historical experience. Many members live in the town of Pillcopata but participate actively in the activities of the community. Even the chief of Queros in 2009 was a person who lived in the town of Pillcopata. There are also people who are not members of the community but for the most part live in Queros, as in the case of the three students and school teacher, who actively participate in community life. Similarly, there are people temporary living away from the community, like students in the city of Cusco and people who are absent for employment reasons, like those working as rangers in the Amarakaeri Community Reserve and the Manu National Park. These people are still considered full members of the community, and sometimes they even perform tasks to benefit the community from their distant locations. Accordingly, the community of Queros should not be understood as a territorially bounded unit but as a network of people whose places of residence transcend a single physical location.

Queros also presents a regular influx of external agents leading to cultural change. Besides people from other ethnolinguistic groups who acquired Wachiperi spouses, in the last two decades the community has received regular visits of people from different organizations. These include the staff of nonprofit organizations implementing development and conservation projects, anthropology and biology students conducting research, government organizations doing infrastructure work, visits from staff from the health center of Pillcopata, tourists visiting the community, people from Pillcopata who own small vehicles and occasionally provide them with cargo transportation services, motorcycle owners from Pillcopata, and others. These interactions have also increased the permeable character of the community borders, where people from other places are increasingly part of the community landscape. As the chief of the community of Queros in 2009 referred to a staff member of an environmental organization who worked as liaison with the community and therefore spent large amounts of time in Queros and Pillcopata, "He is like if he were another member of the community."

Communications is another area that some people of Queros, especially the leaders, are taking advantage of in support of their community projects, like tourism and community-based conservation. Many members of Queros live in the town of Pillcopata, which allows them to have regular access to public telephone and fax services. Several business owners have a messaging service that notifies people who receive telephone calls, for which they charge a small fee. Calls are accessible through many paid telephones in Pillcopata that work with coins and cards. Similarly, postal service is facilitated by the bus lines that connect Pillcopata with the city of Cusco. In addition, the town of Pillcopata has many places where people can rent computers with access to the Internet for an hourly fee. One member of the community of Queros owns one of these Internet places, allowing him to have full access to online communications without any additional costs. This place also attracts the attention of other members of Queros who know how to use computers, especially the young. Two of the most common programs they use are e-mail and instant messaging, allowing them to remain in touch with friends and relatives in other places.

Another important process experienced by the Wachiperi is the instrumental adoption of global discourses, especially the ones related to mainstream conservation and environmental sustainability. This situation has been especially applied to the areas of overlap between the expectations of international conservation organizations to protect biodiversity and the attitudes of the Wachiperi regarding the need to protect the forests and their animal inhabitants. The ancestral values of the Wachiperi, which to some extent are still present in their current environmental behavior, have a significant degree of overlap with the natural resource management expectations of the mainstream organizations supporting the conservation initiatives undertaken by people of Queros. Likewise, the emphasis on the creation of protected areas managed by indigenous peoples overlaps with the desire of the Wachiperi to gain control over the territory of their ancestors, in addition to the Wachiperi goal of protecting those lands from degradation caused by non-indigenous harvesting agents.

People from Queros have become increasingly familiar with the logic of mainstream conservation programs, their funding system, and the possibilities of establishing collaboration mechanisms to have their own concerns addressed, even if they have to learn a new language and adopt a new style of conducting their activities. The experience with their conservation concession in particular has exposed them to a new system of work based on contracts and written terms of reference, management plans, definition of timelines, control of budgets, preparation of reports, and others. Likewise, this involvement has allowed them to become familiar with ideas associated with terms like biodiversity, sustainability, climate change, carbon absorption, conservation corridors, payment for environmental services, deforestation, environmental degradation, surveillance, monitoring, management, donors, and training, among others.

People from Queros have also gained greater knowledge about the legal framework for conservation concessions and natural protected areas in general, the government agencies in charge of specific functions related to the use of the land, among other topics. This new knowledge and their increasing usage has placed the community in a better position to identify opportunities to have their own expectations for social development and environmental conservation fulfilled, especially when done in partnership with organizations that can provide them with technical, financial, and administrative support.

The process where the expectations and practices of local communities are translated into the institutional language and practices of mainstream development and conservation projects has been addressed as "cooption from below" (Mosse 2005: 239). This situation includes the strategies adopted by the local population in relation to external institutions, positioning themselves "within discourses of development, environment, and globalization," and engaging their relationship with nature in innovative terms to support their community claims (Moore et al. 2003: 40). Processes of cooption from below are becoming increasingly common in different parts of the world. In the case of the Wachiperi, this situation is evident in their engagement in community-based conservation, which provides them not only with the means to conserve their natural resources, but also to perceive the potential of natural resources for ecotourism, to provide them with access to the territory of their ancestors, as well as to generate a source of income for members of the community hired as rangers of the conservation concession.

In sum, Wachiperi society has experienced significant changes in the last decades, driving the attention of the younger generation away from subsistence-only practices like hunting toward a combination of subsistence and income-generating activities. These changes have induced the emergence of new needs, desires and consumption habits among the population. Accordingly, cultural change has contributed both to decrease the intensity of hunting practices among the Wachiperi and to increase the adoption of a new way of life based on greater livelihood diversification, especially among the younger generation.

In terms of environmental behavior, their ancestral culture has favored the adoption of sustainable practices, giving precedence to productive activities like tourism and community-based conservation. This is a process not only conducted as an internal affair of this indigenous community, but mainly as a result of their interactions with other actors at local, regional, national and international levels. However, it is also important to acknowledge the crucial importance of local initiatives that enable these larger processes to take place, such as the role played by key individuals like Walter Quertehuari as tourism coordinator, chief of the conservation concession, secretary of the community of Queros, and communications person, among other roles.

Interactions with Outsiders

This section examines the recent establishment of relationships between the community of Queros and external agents, particularly the development of institutional partnerships with external organizations and the political struggles over access to resources in areas neighboring the territory of the community. As Chicchon pointed out, the increasing presence of external social actors has been redefining the characteristics of areas previously occupied only by indigenous peoples (1993: 15), posing a challenge for communities like Queros to address a series of emerging threats and opportunities.

Institutional Partnerships

In the past two decades, the community of Queros has been working toward different development and community-based conservation goals in collaboration with external organizations. The closest ones have been non-government organizations and, to a lesser extent, government agencies. Since the beginning of the 1990s, the community obtained support from the Fundación Peruana para la Conservación de la Naturaleza (Pro-Naturaleza), especially for the establishment of tropical fish farms and community plots to cultivate medicinal plants (Pinasco 2002: 32), in addition to infrastructure projects like the construction of a system to transport water in pipes to the village and improvements to the elementary school. In the middle of the 1990s, the community obtained the support from the Centro para el Desarrollo del Indígena Amazónico (CEDIA) for organizational strengthening and the publication of the Statute of the Community of Queros, a written document that contains the regulations for members of the community and acts as a tool for internal governance.

At the beginning of the 2000s, the Proyecto de Aprovechamiento y Manejo Sostenible de la Reserva de Biosfera del Manu (Pro-Manu) also worked together with people from Queros to develop their environmental management plan, including the design of a community-based ecotourism program. Additional activities were the provision of camping equipment, agricultural extension, and seeds to improve their agricultural practices, the construction of a mini hydroelectric plant, and the improvement of their access road from Pillcopata, among other activities.

After 2005, the Asociación Civil Desarrollo Rural Sustentable (DRIS Peru) also supported the community through the donation of flocks of chickens, expected to be managed as a rotational fund among the different families of Queros after the birds grew up and reproduced. Afterwards, the Asociación Civil de la Reserva de Biosfera del Manu (Sermanu) started working with the community of Queros to develop a new fish farming program, which the Wachiperi reported as successful. Managing fish farms and similar initiatives as a collective was problematic in past experiences, but the community learned that they could get better results when they designated the initial benefits and the responsibility of taking care of the fish to only one family instead of the community as a whole. In a similar way, the community has been working together with The Crees Foundation, which has been bringing groups of tourists to the community, supporting their community-based tourism program.

Since 2007, the Asociación para la Conservación de la Cuenca Amazónica (ACCA) has been providing technical, administrative, and financial support to the community of Queros to manage their conservation concession. They have also been supporting other community development efforts related to their cultural tourism initiative, improvements of the elementary school, training people in different areas, and the construction of a house to be used by the community (see Figure 9). The original purpose of this house was to serve as an office to manage the conservation concession. However, the community has also been using this house as a lodge for visitors, making it a source of collective income. This house has become a visual milestone in the process of obtaining external resources to manage the conservation and tourism projects recently undertaken by the community. As the chief of the conservation concession pointed out, "The concession house is also useful, isn't it? Tourists come there and say in many ways it is better than a hotel."

The Wachiperi have also been working in collaboration with indigenous organizations. The community of Queros is affiliated to the Consejo Harakmbut, Yine y Matsiguenka (COHARYIMA), a local federation that represents the indigenous communities of the Upper Madre de Dios River. In turn, COHARYIMA is a member of the Federación del Rio Madre de Dios y Afluentes (FENAMAD), a regional organization that has continually supported the community of Queros with legal advice about national legislation related to indigenous rights, territorial issues, and many other aspects.

On a larger scale, FENAMAD is a member of the Asociación Interétnica para el Desarrollo de la Selva Peruana (AIDESEP), a national entity that represents regional indigenous organizations and advocates for indigenous rights among government agencies. In turn, AIDESEP is a member of the Coordinadora de Organizaciones Indígenas de la Cuenca Amazónica (COICA), composed of national organizations of nine Amazonian countries, which advocates for indigenous interests at international levels. This structure has facilitated the flow of information across these different levels, a process facilitated by greater access to online communications.

Relationships between the community of Queros and government agencies have been limited to more specific aspects and are much more distant than the ones established with non-government organizations. In terms of the most relevant experiences in the past decade, the municipalities of Paucartambo and Kosñipata provided machinery for the improvement of the access road from Pillcopata, but only on specific occasions. The regional division of the Ministry of Education also provided some funding to replace the roof of the elementary school in Queros. The most stable relationship with a government agency has been with the Servicio Nacional de Áreas Naturales Protegidas (SERNANP), which oversees the conservation concession of the community. As part of their new duties, people from Queros have to prepare management plans and annual reports, and follow up with the status of their paperwork with government officials. This is a long-term relationship, since the conservation concession was granted for a period of forty years. Nevertheless, since the office dealing with concessions is located in Lima, the relationship between members of the community with representatives of SERNANP is for the most part conducted via telephone and email.

The experience of participating in different types of projects with many institutions, especially non-government organizations, has provided the Wachiperi with an opportunity to understand the advantages of this type of collaboration. In the last few years in particular, the community has developed greater capacity to define what type of projects should be pursued, to establish priorities in the planning process, and to negotiate the way the projects are implemented. This enhanced capacity has enabled the acquisition of greater benefits for people in the community, especially through activities that reflect their own expectations about improvements in their living conditions. In relation to hunting, the establishment of relationships with external institutions has to some extent turned their attention away from hunting and toward those activities that have an external counterpart. Externally supported initiatives are combined with their local efforts to present greater potential of satisfying their current needs as in taking care of a fish farm or conducting surveillance activities. Accordingly, institutional partnerships have been moderately influential in decreasing hunting intensity in Queros.

Working in partnership with external institutions has for the most part represented an opportunity that people from Queros have increasingly adopted, which has contributed to the improvement of their living conditions. Improvements are reflected in higher income levels, increased individual self-esteem, significant development of local capacity, stronger sense of cultural identification with the Wachiperi culture, greater diversification of risk in their livelihoods, improved ability to select the type of food consumed, higher sense of overall satisfaction with life than in previous years, and greater optimism about their children's future. Likewise, improvements in their means of transportation from Queros to Pillcopata are also perceived as an important advantage for selling agricultural products and for personal transport. This situation is reflected in the increased use of motorcycles by people in the community, making them less dependent on walking, especially in situations like medical evacuation or when urgent transportation is required. Nevertheless, the relationship between the Wachiperi and external agents has not only been one of cooperation but also of conflict, as is illustrated in the following subsection that describes recent political struggles in the Kosñipata Valley (see Figure 10).

Political Struggles

The period between 2007 and 2008 was characterized by an open conflict between people from the community of Queros and the mayor of Kosñipata. The point of contention was the access to forest areas requested by the community as a conservation concession. The argument raised by the mayor was that people from Queros were being manipulated by the Asociación para la Conservación de la Cuenca Amazónica (ACCA) in an attempt to seize control of those lands, framing his accusations as a matter of access to natural resources. The mayor perceived the presence of the ACCA as a transnational corporation representing foreign interests whose goal was to benefit from the use of the land via the implementation of activities like ecotourism, research centers, and the appropriation of genetic resources, in a similar way to what Katz has addressed as the "privatization of nature" (1998: 48).

In the mayor's view, foreign visitors and biological researchers would become the new authorized users, generating income for the ACCA while the local population remained excluded from this process. The mayor's approach built on current discourses prevalent among peasant movements in the Cusco region, which seemed to be influenced by ideas from dependency theory, anti-capitalism, neocolonialism, anti-globalization, and political regionalism (Quijano 2004). The popularity of these ideas among rural settlers reflects a general discontent with the social order, based on a critical approach to the neoliberal policies implemented by the Peruvian government.

Figure 9. Multipurpose house in the community of Queros

Figure 10. People of Queros protesting against the mayor

One source of discomfort with conservation concessions among rural settlers is fundamentally based on their perceptions of nature. In their view, local natural resources should be used for the benefit of the local population (referring mainly to themselves), as opposed to external organizations, whose mode of operation has historically excluded the local population from the benefits of natural resource exploitation.

These ideas formed the basis of the discourse the mayor used to justify his "attacks" on the communities of Queros and Huacaria, as reported in a regional newspaper (*El Sol* 2009). According to people from Queros, the mayor had threatened these two communities to stop the implementation of projects expected to benefit them if they did not abandon their initiatives with nonprofit organizations. One of the projects reported to be stopped when both communities rejected the threats of the mayor was the abandonment of work on the access roads to both communities. People from Queros claimed that the attitude of the mayor represented an abuse of power.

In this conflict, the mayor had the support of settlers conducting agricultural activities in the rural areas surrounding Pillcopata. Before taking office, the mayor was the president of the Frente Único de Defensa de los Intereses de Kosñipata (FUDIK), which advocated for the rights of loggers to expand their harvesting operations in the area, especially since timber in the Kosnipata Valley was becoming increasingly scarce. FUDIK also supported the claims of coca leaf producers to expand the areas of land available for agricultural production, and to expand the limits imposed by the government on the commercialization of coca leaves. These restrictions led many farmers to support the mayor, with hopes of increased logging and agricultural opportunities.

Beyond the political interests of the mayor, the perception of rural settlers about the land is different than the one of the Wachiperi. In the Andean tradition of settlers, agriculture is the main economic activity and the most important means of subsistence. This situation created a strong attachment to the land among them and a set of values about efficient land use based on intense agricultural productivity.

The land should be allowed a respite only temporarily after having completed a productivity cycle based on rotational crops (Mayer 1994: 518). For settlers with these ideas, setting aside a large portion of land in an "unproductive" or "idle" way, as they perceived conservation concessions, did not make much sense, especially when many people did not have access to agricultural lands. What did make sense for them was the idea of conservation as a strategy of manipulation by external agents to get control of the land to benefit foreign interests. This sense of exclusion provided a propitious space for the mayor of Kosñipata to gain political advantage by adding a rhetorical dimension to these concerns and incorporating them into his political agenda.

One of the specific goals of the mayor was to break the alliance forged between the community of Queros and the ACCA. He perceived the role of nonprofit organizations as external agents who wanted to take control of the land, restricting agricultural expansion and the harvesting of timber, which affected the expectations of rural settlers, the main constituency he represented. The political tensions generated by this conflict between the mayor and the indigenous communities were expressed in different ways. They included mutual accusations of corruption in a public debate broadcasted by the local radio station; a blog discussion where local people on the side of the mayor voiced their opinions in heated tones; and the spread of local rumors that accused the leaders of Queros of being bribed by the ACCA. In response, the community of Queros issued a pronouncement denouncing the harassment conducted by the mayor (Queros and Huacaria 2008), which was electronically distributed among different civil society organizations with the help of the indigenous organization FENAMAD. They also protested in the street during the 2008 anniversary of the Kosñipata District, displaying public signs as shown in Figure 10. People from Queros also reached out to the media in the city of Cusco, and journalists started to look into the issue, raising public concerns about the hostile attitude of the mayor against the indigenous population (*El Sol* 2009: 8).

As the public awareness campaign of people from Queros became increasingly successful, the mayor backed down and changed his attitude. In August 2008, the mayor and the leaders of the community of Queros held a reconciliatory meeting where they agreed to stop all confrontations. Afterwards, the mayor avoided open criticism of both the community of Queros and the ACCA. Nevertheless, his discursive ideological platform remained, especially regarding his opposition to the presence of non-government organizations in the region, the corruption of the national government, and the detrimental role of international entities.

This conflict is evidence of the increasing capacity of people from the community of Queros to stand up to the threats of the district's mayor and conduct a successful public awareness campaign in a way that captured the attention of the regional media. The institutional allies of the community, such as the indigenous organization FENAMAD and the environmental organization ACCA, were also helpful in this process, providing advice and helping people from the community in their struggle with the mayor and his followers. This victory of people from Queros reinforced their sense of cultural identity and increased their collective self-esteem. It also illustrated the importance of allies and friends of the community and the need to continue building a relationship of collaboration with them as an important means of enhancing their own capabilities.

The political struggles with the mayor of Kosñipata also reinforced the decision of the community to continue with the activities related to their conservation concession, adopting the idea not only as a potential alternative, but as a way to prove to the mayor and his followers that the development strategy of the community based on the conservation of the environment works. For now, they have the skeptical attention of people in Pillcopata, most of who still distrust the idea that local people will benefit from conservation. This experience has also reinforced the orientation of the community to pursue sustainable enterprises for their livelihoods. However, their political involvement in community-based conservation has also contributed to driving attention away from traditional activities like hunting, even if the influence of political activities has been manifested in an indirect and moderate way.

Current Ways of Life

The lives of the Wachiperi today are significantly different from what they were five decades ago. Accordingly, our perceptions of their present living conditions should be based on a new way of understanding their reality. This new understanding implies leaving behind stereotypes perpetuated by either inaccurate media reports or theories that are no longer appropriate to explain the present situation of indigenous groups and their environmental behavior. Stereotypes should be replaced by an empirical understanding of social processes on the ground. Likewise, actions should be influenced by a practical understanding of contemporary situations, privileging empirical evidence over rigid theories and models on indigenous environmental behavior.

In the case of the Wachiperi, they have experienced a process of increasing socioeconomic and cultural change. These changes are particularly evident in areas like marriage practices, which have implications for their kinship relations and patterns of residence. The establishment of an elementary school in Queros created changes in people's perceptions of the forest, and also promoted education as a means of upward social mobility in Western society. Likewise, their interaction with external values has created a generational divide between elders and young adults, where the latter have adopted new consumption patterns, transportation practices, and commodified views of the forest. These processes also reflect the presence of globalizing trends, especially when it comes to greater access to communication technologies, human mobility, and the adoption of discourses about mainstream conservation and sustainability.

Deterritorialization is another important process of change experienced in Queros. Accordingly, contemporary indigenous communities should not necessarily be perceived as units bounded by physical limits, but as flexible social networks of people adapting to their changing conditions and linked by a combination of factors like territoriality, formal affiliation, kinship, history, birthright, language, cultural identity, and friendship.

Another important phenomenon that illustrates the changes in Wachiperi society is the recent increase in their interactions with outsiders. Especially relevant are the institutional partnerships built between the community of Queros and non-government environmental organizations, which have had a direct effect on the livelihoods of people in the community and the general lifestyle of the population. Similarly, people from Queros have engaged in political struggles with settlers over issues related to access to land and forest resources, and they have employed novel strategies like reaching out to the regional newspapers, engaging in debates in the local radio, blogs, and walking with protest signs in the middle of the district's anniversary parade (see Figure 10), among others. These activities evidence a greater capacity of people from Queros to access resources outside their community and use them to achieve their community goals.

The changes in community lifestyle previously described illustrate the social conditions that have influenced the diversification of livelihoods among the Wachiperi. These changes include greater familiarity with discourses of Western society that were incorporated in the pursuit of their own aspirations. A similar situation refers to changes in the ways of thinking among people of Queros, especially the younger generation. They have increasingly incorporated Western values, such as the idea of social mobility based on educational achievements, and developed a significantly greater engagement in income-generating activities to satisfy their contemporary needs and desires.

These actions also reflect the importance of agency, or the power of making decisions, which allowed the Wachiperi to explore new opportunities like tourism and environmental conservation. Even with the local opposition of the district's mayor, the Wachiperi pursued innovative paths. They did so based on the advice of young individuals from the community with college educations and greater familiarity with the work of external organizations, and established partnerships with some of them based on their overlapping expectations.

In sum, the socioeconomic transitions experienced by the Wachiperi after they were left with no choice but to establish permanent relationships with members of Western society created a series of dramatic changes in their social landscape, including a decline in the Wachiperi population. These changes transformed their way of life, especially in terms of the establishment of market exchanges with outsiders, which created a transition from a subsistence economy to a mixed economy. After this transition, their engagement in income-generating activities expanded the range of available means of making a living, diversifying their livelihoods and creating new challenges in the allocation of time and effort among their expanded livelihood alternatives. The choices of community members to pursue some activities over others were subsequently influenced by their chances of fulfilling their changing needs for both subsistence and income generation. These decisions were also influenced by the conditions people of Queros experienced as part of their process of cultural change, especially their focus on education as well as the establishment of partnerships with external organizations that supported the initiatives of the community.

Conclusions

After an extensive examination of the different aspects identified as influential in the environmental behavior of the Wachiperi, the conclusion is that the variation in their hunting practices since the middle of the twentieth century was due to a combination of factors like greater diversification in indigenous livelihoods; cultural and ecosystem changes resulting from increased interactions with outsiders; deep social disruptions created by the establishment of closer relationships with members of Western society, including massive deaths from external diseases like smallpox; and the transition from a subsistence economy to a mixed economy. These and other interrelated factors have shaped the current hunting practices of the Wachiperi in a complex way as part of their adaptive experience during the last six decades. This knowledge is important because scholars often disagree about the factors shaping indigenous environmental behavior, which produces competing explanations that influence policies and practices with direct effects on the lives of indigenous peoples.

The ethnographic evidence gathered about the Wachiperi suggests the existence of an inverse relationship: the greater the diversification of livelihoods, the lesser the intensity of hunting practices. Livelihood diversity refers in this case to the existence of socioeconomic activities as alternatives to hunting, which share the allocation of productive resources according to their level of contribution toward the satisfaction of people's needs and desires. In contemporary Wachiperi society, activities that address both subsistence and income-generating purposes, such as agriculture, are increasingly displacing subsistence-only activities like hunting. Their diversification of livelihoods also illustrates that specific activities like hunting are better understood when approached together with other subsistence and income-generating activities carried out by the population. This approach provides a better understanding of the interplay between socioeconomic activities and people's environmental behavior.

The analysis of cross-cultural factors adopted in this book provided an important perspective that allowed me to identify the diversification of livelihoods as one of the most influential proximate causes of variation in hunting intensity among the Wachiperi. As part of this study, the most important aspects identified by scholars as influential in the environmental behavior of indigenous groups in different geographical contexts were succinctly evaluated for the specific case of the Wachiperi. The analysis conducted in Chapter Three identified the diversification of livelihoods as one of the most consistent and recurrent factors influencing hunting intensity. As a first level of analysis in the study of their environmental behavior, the identification of livelihood diversification as one of the most directly influential factors in the hunting practices of the Wachiperi guided the subsequent stages of the analysis.

As a second and intermediate level of analysis, I examined the contemporary changes in the indigenous lifestyle, which contributed to a greater understanding of the current factors affecting different aspects of Wachiperi society, including their hunting practices. Chapters Two and Five illustrate how the adoption of a different lifestyle, which incorporates many cultural elements from Western society, favored the diversification of livelihood alternatives among the Wachiperi. These alternatives, however, have not replaced their traditional activities of subsistence. Instead, the new alternatives coexist with those practiced in previous decades. Livelihood alternatives that emerged in the last decades added a new set of activities to the portfolio of the Wachiperi, expanding the population's range of possibilities.

The recent engagement of the Wachiperi in community-based conservation is an example of this process. While conservation has taken their attention away from hunting, it has not replaced this activity. Instead, conservation has promoted an attitude that allows the Wachiperi to fulfill both their subsistence hunting needs and obtain economic benefits from biodiversity conservation. This situation has favored the incorporation of external elements while maintaining their own cultural specificity. However, a growing trend toward greater articulation to the market economy and the incorporation of Western practices could potentially create further displacement of traditional subsistence activities. This trend can be noticed in activities like logging and tourism, where the generation of monetary income is an important motivation.

The examination of historical processes also provided an extremely valuable analytical perspective as a third level of analysis that addressed the long-term trends in the socioeconomic processes experienced by the Wachiperi. Historical processes contributed to the identification of the root causes of the changes in the intensity of the hunting practices among the Wachiperi. These causes can be traced to the deep social disruptions created by the establishment of closer relationships the Wachiperi had to establish with members of Western society, which generated many deaths among the Wachiperi, changed their settlement patterns, and produced a transition from an economy of subsistence to a mixed economy. A mixed economy (Lu 2007: 601; Tucker 2007: 162) is defined as the coexistence of different productive activities performed on a regular basis, adopted as part of the livelihood of indigenous groups and reflected in the combination of subsistence and market-oriented activities.

A historical perspective also allowed the identification of significant processes that contributed to the shaping of the current situation of the Wachiperi, particularly in the case of the deep social disruptions and deaths created by the introduction of external diseases, the concentration of the Wachiperi into a single settlement, their struggles for access to land, and the movement of settlers into areas near Queros, among other interrelated factors. In addition, a historical perspective allowed me to identify the decline in the intensity of hunting practices among the Wachiperi as a fluctuating process that included temporary increments in the intensity of hunting, especially after the introduction of new hunting technologies like shotguns and flashlights.

At a methodological level, the ethnographic use of the root cause analysis methodology (Steadman-Edwards 1998; Wood et al. 2000) proved to be a powerful analytical framework to understand the variation in hunting intensity at different levels. It combined root causes with proximate causes, integrating different levels of analysis in a coherent way. At the root cause level, the analysis centered on the long-term factors affecting social and environmental conditions, which in the case of the Wachiperi refers to the historical analysis of their experience, particularly the deep social disruptions created by closer interactions with members of Western society and their transition toward a mixed economy. At an intermediate level, the analysis identified the changes in the Wachiperi lifestyle created by their socioeconomic transitions, particularly in terms of cultural change, changes in their food consumption patterns and gender roles, and greater interactions with outsiders. At the proximate level, the analysis focused on the most directly influential factors affecting the hunting practices of the Wachiperi, particularly the diversification of their livelihoods. Thus the ethnographic application of the root cause analysis framework was a good way of organizing all these different influential factors in a coherent way, providing me with a comprehensive understanding of the variation in hunting intensity among the Wachiperi.

In relation to the implications of changes in the intensity of Wachiperi hunting practices for the biological diversity of the area, the evidence gathered indicates that there was not a causal relationship between these variables. The Wachiperi recalled that game was significantly more abundant in the middle of the twentieth century, both in terms of the number of species and the populations within each species. The abundance of game coincided with a very high level of hunting by the Wachiperi, who at the time lived scattered throughout the Kosñipata Valley. This situation suggests an association between high levels of hunting and high biodiversity in the middle of the twentieth century. Today, the levels of hunting are lower and biodiversity is scarcer in Queros. Accordingly, the argument that higher levels of indigenous hunting result in decreased availability of forest animals does not apply to the case of the Wachiperi.

The decrease in the intensity of Wachiperi hunting practices in the last five decades has not created an increase in biodiversity. On the contrary, many species have become scarcer over time. This scarcity is mainly the result of increased human migration to the area, since in the last few decades numerous settlers have been farming, logging, and hunting commercially, disturbing the local forests and their animal inhabitants. This decline in the area's biodiversity has been mainly the result of the neighboring settlers' activities that negatively impact the area's biodiversity, rather than the result of indigenous hunting. As an elderly Wachiperi man described it to me, the fact that people from Queros do not hunt frequently these days has encouraged, in some cases, settlers to go hunting within the territory of Queros, since there is little chance of these poachers running into people from Queros and being chased away.

Thus indigenous communities should not be perceived in isolation but in relation to the non-indigenous population living close to their territories. This situation illustrates that in some cases the focus on the hunting practices of indigenous groups as drivers of biodiversity loss has been misplaced, especially because it ignores the effects of non-indigenous neighbors and other socioeconomic processes. In the Kosñipata Valley, activities such as agricultural expansion, logging, commercial hunting, and butterfly catching have been conducted with greater intensity by settlers.

Regarding the implications of a reduction in the intensity of hunting on the living conditions of the Wachiperi, the decrease in their hunting practices has been directly related to the emergence of new opportunities for socioeconomic development and local capacity building. Activities like commercial agriculture, small-scale logging, and cultural tourism have increasingly displaced subsistence-only activities like hunting. At the same time, they have promoted higher levels of education, stronger community organization and sense of cultural identity, greater diversification of risks and food security, greater access to monetary income, better communication technologies, means of transportation, and improved local infrastructure.

The Wachiperi are also benefitting from the recent adoption of a development strategy based on environmental sustainability. They understand conservation as a goal in itself, but also as a means for development. The recent engagement of the Wachiperi in community-based conservation has favored the establishment of partnerships with environmental organizations, based on the overlap of their mutual expectations, which have provided people of Queros with an important influx of monetary resources and opportunities for local capacity building. However, there have also been negative effects in this process. For example, the emergence of new needs and desires among the Wachiperi has increasingly generated greater dependence on outside resources as well as greater risks of internal differentiation between members of Queros, especially in terms of access to monetary income and level of education. Other related risks for the Wachiperi include an increase in chronic health problems, soil degradation, conflicts with outsiders, internal political tensions, and loss of cultural traditions and ancestral knowledge.

The Wachiperi are aware of the risks and problems created by the rapid process of social change and engagement in market activities. This awareness has led them to reflect on the need to create spaces for the reproduction of their ancestral culture, including values, beliefs, knowledge, and perceptions of the forest. Cultural reproduction is increasingly important to them as a way of keeping a connection with their traditions in a rapidly changing world. The diversification of livelihoods has contributed to a decrease in the intensity of hunting practices and has provided the Wachiperi with new opportunities to improve their living conditions but at the same time has generated new risks and problems. This is an area of rising concern for them.

In the long term, however, the self-determined focus on sustainability, education, community organization, and recovery of cultural traditions is likely to place the Wachiperi in a better position than similar groups lacking these characteristics, especially if they create social spaces to reflect on the direction of their socioeconomic changes and develop mechanisms to mitigate their potentially harmful effects. However, it is important to clarify that the experience of the Wachiperi has been defined by a set of favorable conditions that are not representative of other indigenous groups in the Peruvian Amazon or other rain forest environments. Other groups have not had the same opportunities but instead a series of structural forces and devastating events leading to the degradation of their living conditions.

At a more general level, the experience of the Wachiperi suggests that livelihood diversification could be a critical factor in the analysis of indigenous environmental behavior. While its relevance may vary in different geographical and cultural settings, livelihood diversification could also be an important process among other indigenous groups that experienced similar transitions toward a mixed economy. The expansion of the global economy, which is increasingly reaching indigenous communities on a global scale, is likely promoting transitions to mixed economies. However, this possibility should be confirmed at a practical level. Whether or not livelihood diversification is relevant to understand the environmental behavior of other indigenous groups should be a matter of empirical evaluation.

The effect of livelihood diversification on the environmental behavior of the Wachiperi also provides important insight into the socioeconomic and environmental motivations of indigenous groups to conserve biodiversity, revealing the need to address these concerns together. Similarly, the analysis of the variation in Wachiperi hunting practices supports the idea that indigenous environmental behavior depends on the adaptive living conditions of each population. This situation is illustrated by the process of livelihood diversification, which has been influential in shaping the recent socioeconomic and environmental activities of the Wachiperi, especially as they became engaged in a combination of subsistence practices and market activities. Diversification of livelihoods was thus revealed as a factor with great potential of contribution to understanding the environmental behavior of indigenous groups living in tropical forests.

The analysis indicates that the engagement of indigenous groups in a mixed economy creates changes in their lifestyle that require the development of different sets of skills to satisfy the new needs and desires created by regular market exchanges. In the case of people from Queros, they adopted a strategy based on the development of capacities among its members, which placed them in an optimal position to take advantage of the emerging opportunities available to them, increasing the range of choices in terms of livelihoods. Spending their scarce earnings on the education of young people has proven to be a rewarding investment, since members of the community with a college education have been playing a critical role in generating new opportunities for the improvement of the living conditions of the group. They are helping the community run its cultural tourism program, negotiating partnerships with external organizations, attracting financial resources, and developing a network of friends and allies to support the community in different areas, such as their political struggles with settlers and the preparation of technical documents, among many other actions.

Individuals from the community with a college education have also obtained professional jobs with higher salaries and social status, such as chief of the conservation concession and director of the secondary school in Pillcopata, the capital of the Kosñipata district. These positions have enhanced the confidence of the Wachiperi as a group in relation to settlers, creating new role models, producing their own social discourses, and strengthening their sense of cultural identity. Accordingly, the experience of people from Queros could serve as a reference for other cases as well, especially if the focus on education is not limited to young people but is extended to basic literacy and general education for every person in the community, both women and men.

In addition to capacity development, indigenous communities could benefit from defining a long-term perspective on their choices for livelihoods that includes a socioeconomic and environmental sustainability dimension to their income-generating activities. In the case of the Wachiperi, sustainable socioeconomic alternatives like community-based conservation and tourism are already producing benefits in the short term, but the positive impacts in the long term could be even greater if they maintain the present course of action. Sustainable alternatives are expected to be especially relevant in areas with declining agricultural production rates, such as in the community of Queros and its surroundings, which in the next few decades are likely to be affected by factors like loss of the natural fertility of the soil, the presence of new agricultural pests, and the pollution created by artificial fertilizers, pesticides, and herbicides. In time, the use of these products could increase costs and decrease profits.

Logging without a systematic reforestation program is also an unsustainable enterprise that, beyond its temporary cash benefits, is likely to continue losing economic importance in the following decades, especially as commercial timber species become scarce. Therefore, indigenous groups could benefit from avoiding over reliance on unsustainable activities like logging and commercial agriculture. Exploring the potential benefits of sustainable enterprises could provide steadier benefits in the long term, both in terms of subsistence activities and the generation of income, such as the community-based conservation and tourism in the case of the Wachiperi.

In the process of introducing a sustainability criterion in their income-generating activities, some indigenous communities might find this initial transition challenging. Enlisting the support of external parties could be a useful strategy as a temporary stage until communities can strengthen their own capacity and become more autonomous to follow the path of their choice. Likely parties in this process are mainstream conservation and development nonprofits, which are increasingly recognizing the value of establishing partnerships with indigenous communities in areas where their mutual expectations overlap. However, indigenous groups should also be wary and skeptical about external organizations, especially at the beginning of their interactions with them. Missionary groups in particular should be dealt with cautiously, since their expectations to modify indigenous behavior based on external values may lead to cultural imposition, external dependency, and social disruption, as was the case of the Wachiperi before they distanced themselves from the missionaries.

The experience of the Wachiperi is an example of how communities can take the initiative and approach external institutions in search of potential areas of collaboration. When a potential match is identified, one of the first goals should be the establishment of a relationship between representatives of the community and the nonprofit organization. This relationship should be built in a progressive way, based on the principles of transparency, mutual trust, and equal respect that should be observed by all parties, setting the initial expectations low and adjusting them as interactions evolve. Additional likely partners could be other indigenous communities engaged in similar processes, where the exchange of experiences might contribute to thinking of new ways to achieve community goals. This exchange could also provide some level of comfort in knowing that other indigenous groups are going through similar experiences, exploring new opportunities, and adapting as best as they can to cope with the demands of a changing world. While the process of building partnerships with external organizations may generate some local opposition, and in some cases even create political struggles, indigenous groups should stand for what they feel is right according to their particular circumstances. The advice of settlers should be followed with caution, since their views of the forest and the use of natural resources are likely to be different.

Another important process would be to develop internal mechanisms to prevent or reduce the negative social impacts of changes in the indigenous lifestyle as a result of their engagement in market-oriented activities. For instance, changes in food consumption patterns with significant increases in sugars, carbohydrates, and fried foods, together with a reduction in the usual levels of physical exercise, could lead to the generation of chronic illnesses like diabetes, hypertension, anemia, obesity, and cardiovascular and heart diseases. In a similar way, improvements in the conditions of the local roads could bring not only benefits, such as greater facility to sell agricultural products, but also considerable risks. Ecological risks are also important, such as habitat fragmentation, which may reduce the availability of forest animals in the area, especially when secondary branches of the main roads are opened. Social risks include a greater presence of settlers seeking to expand the frontier of their logging operations, poachers, furtive fishers, gold miners, thieves, and others whose harvesting activities may create situations of conflict when confronted by the indigenous population. Greater awareness of these and other potential risks could help indigenous communities develop a monitoring system to allow them to anticipate potentially negative impacts and take measures to prevent or reduce their intensity according to the nature of the problem. The creation of institutional spaces in the community for the discussion of potential risks and the need to take action could be significant in this process as well.

In terms of the relationship between men and women, the recent engagement of the Wachiperi in tourism illustrates that indigenous groups can make greater progress toward their community goals when women and men work together. Wider participation and equitable distribution of benefits, regardless of gender, could contribute to better conditions for the ownership and success of community projects. Beyond tourism, the contribution of men and women could be expanded to other areas society and could improve their performing potential for community development.

At a theoretical level, this research was grounded on an empirical approach that favored the use of practical evidence while also incorporating elements from multiple theoretical traditions in a transparadigmatic and eclectic way. This approach fit well with the study of social phenomena from a multilevel and flexible perspective. The appropriateness of this flexible approach became clearer after completing the literature review for this research project, which defined this approach as an adequate alternative to overcome both essentialist assumptions and unrealistic models that have significantly influenced the academic debates about the relationship between indigenous peoples and tropical biodiversity.

The ethnographic application of the root cause analysis framework allowed me to integrate multiple levels of analysis, incorporate elements from different theoretical traditions in a coherent fashion, organize different types of information, facilitate the analysis of complex ethnographic data, and provide a comprehensive understanding of the topic explored. As such, I recommend the ethnographic application of this analytical framework not only in the study of indigenous environmental behavior, but also in other anthropological endeavors where multiple factors and levels of analysis need to be taken into account in the search for holistic explanations about the underlying causes of social phenomena.

Another important reflection regarding the use of anthropology to advocate for social and environmental justice is that there should be a significant concern for empirical understanding first as a necessary intermediate point between theory and action. The absence of clear mechanisms to promote the abandonment of theoretical assumptions when they do not apply to particular cases has led me to perceive the risks of a potential disconnect between theory and practice, which could lead to situations where theories act mainly as a source of bias. This type of theoretical bias could prevent an adequate understanding of the complexity of reality, especially in areas that present new types of social dynamics that were not anticipated at the time the theories were developed. To varying degrees, acting solely on the basis of theoretical assumptions could lead to an essentialist view of reality. Accordingly, I suggest that the adoption of attitudes and practices intended to bring about social change should strive to achieve a comprehensive understanding of the socioenvironmental processes happening on the ground first.

In terms of gender considerations, the experience of the Wachiperi suggests that the study of hunting should not be addressed as solely a male activity. The examination of the role of women in hunting proved to be very insightful in terms of understanding the complexity of this practice, illustrating the diffuse borders, interconnections, and collaboration across genders that enabled men to perform their hunting roles. The roles of men also acquired a new dimension when understood in terms of their relationship with the productive roles of women. The livelihoods approach to gender roles adopted in this study encouraged me to perceive the activities of men and women not as separate and mutually exclusive, but as linked in complementary ways, revealing crucial elements of analysis that I could have missed otherwise. As such, I recommend a similar awareness in the study of hunting and other productive activities that the literature or conventional wisdom portray as the exclusive domain of either men or women.

In relation to environmental organizations, a policy suggestion is that they should make greater efforts to involve indigenous peoples as partners in conservation. The experience of the Wachiperi reinforces the idea that productive alliances are possible when they are based on the mutual overlap of expectations between indigenous groups and environmental organizations. When properly motivated, indigenous groups are among the best suited to apply their skills to achieve conservation results on the ground, particularly against the threats posed by non-indigenous individuals and organizations. These skills include their ancestral knowledge, contemporary training, adaptability to changing circumstances, legitimacy provided by ancestral domain, and willingness to engage in political struggles with outsiders to protect the territory of their ancestors from environmental degradation. However, the opportunity costs of actively engaging in grassroots conservation activities is high, since their engagement in a mixed economy has created the need for monetary income to satisfy their contemporary needs and desires, as in the case of the Wachiperi.

In this context, competitive economic incentives are likely to decrease the opportunity costs of grassroots conservation, providing indigenous peoples with an adequate motivation to conserve their forests and local biological diversity in addition to the non-monetary benefits of conservation for the communities. Likewise, logistical support and regular training are key aspects in facilitating the acquisition of indigenous peoples' abilities to work effectively in institutional work styles, which are largely dependent on management systems based on written documents. While the process of establishing partnerships with indigenous communities may be long and slow-paced at the beginning, in the long term it is likely to achieve effective results. Accordingly, environmental organizations should strive to engage indigenous communities as partners in community-based conservation, providing economic incentives and institutional support to facilitate the implementation of joint conservation projects.

In the process of building partnerships with indigenous communities, the focus could be on the development of local capacity for community-based conservation. This should be a comprehensive effort through activities like providing college scholarships for indigenous students, whose education would later enable them to contribute more effectively to environmental conservation. Also important would be to provide training for the population in areas directly related to conservation, including communications, management, leadership, financial accountability, computer literacy, and social and environmental monitoring, among others. In addition, the development of practical conservation management skills would be important. This could be achieved by transferring to community representatives the ability to implement programs themselves, according to management plans, which should be developed in a collaborative way between representatives of the communities and the staff of environmental organizations.

In the case of the Wachiperi, the environmental organization supporting them (ACCA) maintained financial accountability of the monetary funds, but a community representative took charge of the implementation of the funds. This modality was favored by the technical advice of a staff member of the ACCA designated as community liaison, who ensured compliance with institutional procedures, especially in the preparation of budgets and technical reports. In this process, indigenous communities that develop the capacity for environmental management, especially those with college-educated members, should be progressively trusted with increasing responsibilities in the design and implementation of projects. The goal should be the development of a collaborative relationship aimed at creating greater autonomy among indigenous communities to conserve biodiversity. Accordingly, the development of local capacity among indigenous groups should be addressed as an important conservation investment.

The focus on capacity building among indigenous communities is based on the idea that conservation strategies in general should be multidimensional, and articulate socioeconomic and environmental aspects. Even if the main goal is conserving biodiversity, the multiple dimensions of environmental processes create the need to address the different parts of the problem. Accordingly, research priorities should not be limited to ecological processes, but extended to include the socioeconomic processes associated with them. This requires the appropriate allocation of funds for research on the social, cultural, political, and economic causes of environmental outcomes and processes.

In addition, mainstream conservation actions should not be limited to addressing environmental concerns alone, but should also include the socioeconomic aspects of conservation. These aspects refer to community organization, training on environmental management practices, economic incentives for conservation, the recovery of those cultural traditions that encourage conservation, and other aspects expected to strengthen the local capacity for conservation. The inclusion of the socioeconomic concerns of the indigenous population would also contribute to improvements in their living conditions and increase the levels of collective motivation and local ownership of conservation projects, as illustrated by the experience of the Wachiperi in the management of their conservation concession. Their experience suggests that closer integration between socioeconomic and environmental concerns is likely to produce greater effectiveness in long-term conservation, as well as to promote higher levels of commitment among the indigenous population.

My experience in this research project also suggests that environmental organizations should strive to develop conservation policies based on a solid understanding of the socioeconomic and environmental conditions on the ground. Historical processes and events with significant impacts on the lives of indigenous peoples should be included in this understanding, and empirical evidence should be central to determining mainstream conservation interventions. In this process, the ethnographic application of the root cause analysis methodology provides an effective means of guiding such research endeavors. This analytical framework could help organize complex social information in a concise way and facilitate the decision-making process. However, the task of gathering, processing, and analyzing the right socioeconomic information requires the involvement of qualified social practitioners. This requirement could be fulfilled by increasing the percentage of social scientists among the permanent staff of environmental organizations, especially in cases where professional expertise is mainly constituted by conservation biologists and other life scientists. Social scientists could be systematically included as team members in mainstream conservation projects and programs, providing advice on the adoption and implementation of conservation policies and practices and facilitating the process of establishing mutually fulfilling partnerships with indigenous groups.

When implementing conservation projects on the ground, the way practitioners frame their understanding of the relationship between indigenous peoples and tropical biodiversity influence their decisions about the type of activities to be conducted. Understanding indigenous peoples as adaptive agents reduces the risk of essentializing their environmental behavior. The actions of practitioners should be based on an empirical understanding of the causes of variation in indigenous environmental behavior, as well as the behavior of non-indigenous individuals and organizations, instead of an over-reliance on theories or models that only offer general explanations. A nuanced understanding of what is happening on the ground is critical in the search for information and should not be substituted for general theoretical assumptions. Failure to achieve an empirical understanding before undertaking any type of conservation projects may lead to interventions that overlook important trends, especially emerging social processes that may be beneficial or detrimental to environmental conservation. Reliable information is more likely to help anticipate socioeconomic trends, define the direction of actions intended to support or consolidate community processes leading to conservation, and guide the decision-making process according to the specific needs of particular contexts.

When assessing the social aspects likely to affect conservation in a given setting, it is important to examine not only the proximate causes of the social and environmental processes examined, but also the larger socioeconomic causes behind the observable conditions. In the case of the Wachiperi, this was achieved by understanding livelihood diversification within the context of their historical processes, their evolving social roles, and their process of sociocultural change, among other factors. While the specific conditions of a particular setting may call for different configurations and the identification of specific factors and processes, acknowledging that proximate causes are the result of larger processes is important and should be included in the analysis. In a similar way, the different causes of social and environmental processes should not be understood and treated in an isolated way. Instead, they should be framed in a way that recognizes their connections with other relevant factors as well as their reciprocal interactions at different levels. These practices would introduce the basic elements of a more holistic approach to the analysis of socioenvironmental processes, contribute to a greater understanding of their complexity, and increase the chances of achieving effective conservation.

In a more practical sense, when working with indigenous groups it is important to develop management plans beyond the confines of their communities. As in the case of the Wachiperi, the role of neighboring settlers has been significantly more influential than the one of people from Queros in affecting the availability of forest animals in the area. In similar cases, plans that include the role of outsiders in the core of the problem are more likely to create positive changes than plans that focus exclusively on the environmental practices of people in the indigenous communities. Members of indigenous communities living outside their villages should also be included as critical players. Similarly, the interactions between indigenous peoples and outsiders are likely to affect the way indigenous communities behave. Political conflicts and regional struggles for land may affect the direction of community-based conservation initiatives in significant ways. Also, the establishment of partnerships between indigenous communities and environmental organizations may increase the possibility of successful results. In sum, interactions with outsiders should be included as a key factor in the planning process, which should be conducted in collaboration with indigenous groups and should reflect their concerns. These concerns must include indigenous expectations of economic incentives, the development of local capacity for conservation and development, and the conservation of local forests and their animal inhabitants.

These lessons and recommendations are expected to increase the chances of success in community-based conservation. They seek to promote socially and environmentally sustainable solutions that are both effective for long-term biodiversity conservation and socially beneficial for the indigenous population. Greater understanding of the factors shaping indigenous environmental behavior is expected to guide better decision-making processes, as well as generate greater opportunities for the improvement of the living conditions of indigenous groups. Adopting a holistic perspective in the analysis is also a very important step in the process of contributing to the adoption of more socially inclusive and environmentally just conservation strategies when working with indigenous peoples.

References

Alvard, Michael
1995   Intraspecific Prey Choice by Amazonian Hunters.
        Current Anthropology 36 (5): 789–818.

Andrade, Regis, Alfredo Ugarte, Crayla Alfaro, Chabuca
Condorpusa, and Guillermina Huanca
2006   Diagnóstico Socio-Cultural de la Etnia Huachiperi.
        Technical report. Cusco, Perú: Instituto Nacional de
        Cultura, Centro Regional para la Salvaguarda del
        Patrimonio Cultural Inmaterial para América Latina,
        and Municipalidad Distrital de Kcosñipata.

Appadurai, Arjun
2003   Global Ethnoscapes: Notes and Queries for a
        Transnational Anthropology. *In* Recapturing
        Anthropology: Working in the Present. Richard Fox, ed.
        Pp. 191–209. Santa Fe, NM: School of American
        Research Press.

Balée, William and Clark Erickson, eds.
2006   Time and Complexity in Historical Ecology: Studies in
        the Neotropical Lowlands. New York: Columbia
        University Press.

Barriales, Joaquín and Adolfo Torralba
1970   Los Mashcos: Hijos del Huanamei. Lima, Perú:
        Secretariado de Misiones Dominicanas.

171

Bedoya, Andres
2009   ¡Pobrecitos Chunchos! y Otras Torpezas. Article in the
       Peruvian newspaper *Correo*, published on June 13, 2009.
       http://www.correoperu.com.pe/correo/columnistas.p
       hp?txtEdi_id=4&txtSecci_parent=&txtSecci_id=84&txtN
       ota_id=73466, accessed October 14, 2009.

Berkes, Fikret
2004   Rethinking Community-Based Conservation.
       Conservation Biology 18 (3): 621–630.

Berkes, Fikret and Carl Folke, eds.
1998 Linking Social and Ecological Systems for Resilience and
       Sustainability. *In* Linking Social and Ecological Systems:
       Management Practices and Social Mechanisms for
       Building Resilience. Pp. 1–25. Cambridge: Cambridge
       University Press.

Califano, Mario
1982   Etnografía de los Mashco de la Amazonía Sud
       Occidental del Perú. Buenos Aires, Argentina: FECIE.
1985   El Tema de la Guerra entre los Mashco de la Amazonía
       Sudoccidental (Perú). Scripta Ethnologica 9: 7–23.

Chernela, Janet
2005   The Politics of Mediation: Local-Global Interactions in
       the Central Amazon of Brazil. American Anthropologist
       107 (4): 620–631.

Chicchon, Avecita
1993   El Uso de la Fauna en la Amazonía: Los Límites de la
       Sostenibilidad. Arequipa, Perú: Seminario Permanente
       de Investigación Agraria V.

Clay, Jason
1988 Indigenous Peoples and Tropical Forests: Models of
      Land Use and Management from Latin America.
      Cambridge, MA: Cultural Survival.

Colchester, Marcus
1994 Salvaging Nature: Indigenous Peoples, Protected Areas
      and Biodiversity. Discussion paper 55. Geneva: United
      Nations Research Institute for Social Development,
      World Rain Forest Movement and World Wide Fund.

Contreras, Violeta
2007 Diagnóstico Social Actualizado de la Comunidad Nativa
      de Queros. Technical report. Cusco, Perú: Asociación
      para la Conservación de la Cuenca Amazónica.

El Sol
2009 Miles lo Rechazan: Alcalde de Kosñipata Odia a los
      Nativos. Cusco, Perú: Diario El Sol, July 9: 8.

Ellis, Frank
2000 Rural Livelihoods and Diversity in Developing
      Countries. New York: Oxford University Press.

Escalante, Carmen and Ricardo Valderrama
2000 Documentos Históricos y Memoria Colectiva sobre el
      Uso de la Biodiversidad en la Reserva de Biosfera del
      Manu. Institutional report. Cusco, Peru: Pro-Manu.

Estioko-Griffin, Agnes
1993 Daughters of the Forest. *In* The Other Fifty Percent:
      Multicultural Perspectives on Gender Relations. Mari
      Womack and Judith Marti, eds. Pp. 225–232. Prospect
      Heights, IL: Waveland Press.

Fernández, Wenceslao
1952   Cincuenta Años en la Selva Amazónica: Padres
       Dominicos Españoles. Puerto Maldonado, Perú:
       Vicariato de Puerto Maldonado.

Giddens, Anthony
1984   The Constitution of Society: Outline of the Theory of
       Structuration. Berkeley: University of California Press.

Hall, Anthony
1997   Sustaining Amazonia: Grassroots Action for Productive
       Conservation. New York: Manchester University Press.

Harvey, David
1996   Justice, Nature and the Geography of Difference.
       Cambridge, MA: Blackwell Publishers.

Helberg, Heinrich
1987   Descripción y Documentación de una Lengua
       Amazónica del Perú: Harakmbut Hate. Unpublished
       MS. Lima, Peru: Universidad Nacional de San Marcos.
1996   MBAISIK en la Penumbra del Atardecer: Literatura Oral
       del Pueblo Harakmbut. Lima, Peru: CAAAP.

Hofer, Heribert, Kenneth Campbell, M. East and Sally Huish
1996   The Impact of Game Meat Hunting on Target and Non-
       target Species in the Serengeti. *In* The Exploitation of
       Mammal Populations. Victoria Taylor and Nigel
       Dunstone, eds. Pp. 117–146. London, UK: Chapman and
       Hall.

Holmberg, Allan
1969   Nomads of the Long Bow: The Siriono of Eastern
       Bolivia. Garden City, NY: Natural History Press.

Igoe, James
2004   History, Culture and Conservation: In Search of More
       Informed Guesses about whether "Community-based
       Conservation" has a Chance to Work. Policy Matters 13
       (November): 174–185.
2005   Global Indigenism and Spaceship Earth: Convergence,
       Space, and Re-entry Friction. Globalizations 2 (3): 377–
       390.

Igoe, James and Crystal Fortwangler
2007   Introduction: Whither communities and conservation?
       International Journal of Biodiversity Science and
       Management 3: 1–12.

Inrena
2008   Estado Peruano Otorga Primera Concesión de
       Conservación a Comunidad Nativa del Cusco. Instituto
       Nacional de Recursos Naturales. Electronic document,
       http://www.inrena.gob.pe/comunicaciones/notas_por
       tada/nota080703-1.htm, accessed July 3, 2008.

Katz, Cindy
1998   Whose Nature, Whose Culture? Private Productions of
       Space and the "Preservation" of Nature. *In* Remaking
       Reality: Nature at the Millennium. Bruce Braun and
       Noel Castree, eds. Pp. 46–63. New York: Routledge.

Kirby, Kris, Ricardo Godoy, Victoria Reyes-García, Elizabeth
Byron, Lilian Apaza, William Leonard, Eddy Pérez, Vincent
Vadez, and David Wilkie
2002   Correlates of Delay-Discount Rates: Evidence from
       Tsimane' Amerindians of the Bolivian Rain Forest.
       Journal of Economic Psychology 23 (3): 291–316.

Lamoreux, John, John Morrison, Taylor Ricketts, David Olson, Eric Dinerstein, Meghan Mcknight, and Herman Shugart
2007   The Multifaceted Nature of Biodiversity Conservation: Reply to Leroux and Schmiegelow. Conservation Biology 21 (1): 269–270.

Lathrap, Donald
1973   The "Hunting" Economies of the Tropical Forest Zone of South America: An Attempt at Historical Perspective. *In* Peoples and Cultures of Native South America. Daniel Gross, ed. Pp. 83–95. Garden City, NY: Natural History Press.

Little, Paul
1999   Environments and Environmentalisms in Anthropological Research: Facing a New Millennium. Annual Review of Anthropology 28: 253–284.

Lleellish, Miguel, Juan Ayala, Jose Manzur, and Miriam Matorela
2007   El Circuito de Comercialización y los Procesos de Valor Agregado de Pieles de Pecaríes. Technical report, Instituto Nacional de Recursos Naturales. Lima, Perú.

Llosa, Eliana and Luis Nieto
2003   El Manu a Través de la Historia. Cusco, Perú: Pro-Manu.

Lu, Flora
2007   Integration into the Market among Indigenous Peoples: A Cross-Cultural Perspective from the Ecuadorian Amazon. Current Anthropology 48 (4): 593–602.

Lyon, Patricia
1967   Singing as Social Interaction among the Wachipaeri of Eastern Peru. PhD dissertation. Graduate Division, University of California, Berkeley.

1975   Dislocación Tribal y Clasificaciones Lingüísticas en la
       Zona del Rio Madre de Dios. Lima, Perú: XXXIX
       Congreso Internacional de Americanistas.

Martinez-Alier, Joan
2002   The Environmentalism of the Poor: A Study of
       Ecological Conflicts and Valuation. Northampton, MA:
       Edward Elgar Publishing.

Mascia-Lees, Frances and Nancy Johnson Black
2000   Gender and Anthropology. Prospect Heights, IL:
       Waveland Press.

Mayer, Enrique
1994   Recursos Naturales, Medio Ambiente, Tecnología y
       Desarrollo. *In* Perú: El Problema Agrario en Debate.
       Oscar Dancourt, Enrique Mayer, Carlos Monge, eds. Pp.
       479–533. Lima, Perú. SEPIA / UNSA / CAPRODA.

Meggers, Betty
1971   Amazonia: Man and Culture in a Counterfeit Paradise.
       Chicago: Aldine-Atherton.

Moore, Donald, with Anand Pandian and Jake Kosek, eds.
2003   The Cultural Politics of Race and Nature: Terrains of
       Power and Practice. *In* Race, Nature, and the Politics of
       Difference. Pp. 1–70. Durham, NC: Duke University
       Press.

Moore, Thomas
1979   SIL and a "New-found tribe": The Amarakaeri
       Experience. Dialectical Anthropology 4 (2): 113–125.

Mosse, David
2005   Cultivating Development: An Ethnography of Aid
       Policy and Practice. Ann Arbor, MI: Pluto Press.

Narayan, Deepa
1998   Participatory Rural Development. *In* Agriculture and
       the Environment: Perspectives on Sustainable Rural
       Development. Ernst Lutz, ed. Pp. 103–117. Washington,
       DC: The World Bank.

Oates, John
2000   Why a Prime Model for Saving Rain Forests Is a Failure.
       The Chronicle of Higher Education 46 (19): B6.

Ohl, Julia, Alexander Wezel, Glenn Shepard, and Douglas Yu
2008   Swidden Agriculture in a Protected Area: The
       Matsiguenka Native Communities of Manu National
       Park, Peru. Environment, Development and
       Sustainability 10 (6): 827–843.

Peacock, Nadine
1991   Rethinking the Sexual Division of Labor: Reproduction
       and Women's Work among the Efe. *In* Gender at the
       Crossroads of Knowledge: Feminist Anthropology in
       the Postmodern Era. Micaela di Leonardo, ed. Pp.
       339–360. Berkeley: University of California Press.

Pinasco, Karina
2002   Participación Comunitaria en la Elaboración del Plan de
       Manejo Ambiental de la Comunidad Nativa de Queros –
       Zona de Transición Amazónica de la Reserva de
       Biosfera del Manu. Lima, Perú. M.S. Thesis. Escuela de
       Post-Grado, Universidad Nacional Agraria La Molina.

Pinedo, Donaldo
2008   Diagnóstico Social de la Comunidad Nativa de Queros,
       Actualizado y Validado. Technical report. Cusco, Perú:
       Asociación para la Conservación de la Cuenca
       Amazónica / Comunidad Nativa de Queros.

Posey, Darrell
1998   Diachronic Ecotones and Anthropogenic Landscapes in
       Amazonia: Contesting the Consciousness of
       Conservation. *In* Advances in Historical Ecology.
       William Balée, ed. Pp. 104–118. New York: Columbia
       University Press.

Queros, Comunidad Nativa
1996   Estatuto de la Comunidad Nativa de Queros: Aprobado
       en Asamblea General Extraordinaria del 11 de Octubre
       de 1995. Lima, Peru: Centro para el Desarrollo del
       Indígena Amazónico.

Queros and Huacaria
2008   Pronunciamiento: Las Comunidades Nativas del Valle
       de Kosñipata Denuncian el Constante Atropello de sus
       Derechos. Pillcopata, Perú: Electronic document,
       http://www.queros.net/selva-
       peru/2008/03/pronunciamiento-indigena-
       derechos.html, accessed November 21, 2008.

Quijano, Anibal
2004   Colonialidad del Poder, Eurocentrismo y América
       Latina. *In* Globalización y Diversidad Cultural: Una
       Mirada desde América Latina. Ramón Pajuelo and
       Pablo Sandoval, eds. Pp. 228–281. Lima, Perú: Instituto
       de Estudios Peruanos.

Redford, Kent and Steven Sanderson
2000   Extracting Humans from Nature. Conservation Biology
       14 (5): 1362–1364.

Robinson, John, Kent Redford, and Elizabeth Bennett
1999   Wildlife Harvest in Logged Tropical Forests. Science
       284: 595–596.

Russell, Diane and Camilla Harshbarger
 2003   Groundwork for Community-Based Conservation:
        Strategies for Social Research. Walnut Creek, CA:
        Altamira Press.

Santos, Fernando
 1985   Crónica Breve de un Etnocidio o Génesis del Mito del
        Gran Vacío Amazónico. Amazonía Peruana 6 (11): 9–38.
        Lima, Perú.

Siskind, Janet
 1973   Tropical Forest Hunters and the Economy of Sex. *In*
        Peoples and Cultures of Native South America. Daniel
        Gross, ed. Pp. 226–240. Garden City, NY: Natural
        History Press.

Slocum, Sally
 2004 [1975] Woman the Gatherer: Male Bias in Anthropology.
        In Anthropological Theory: An Introductory History.
        John McGee and Richard Warms, eds. Pp. 476–484. New
        York: McGraw Hill.

Smith, Eric and Mark Wishnie
 2000   Conservation and Subsistence in Small-Scale Societies.
        Annual Review of Anthropology 29: 493–524.

Stange, Mary
 1997   Woman the Hunter. Boston, MA: Beacon Press Books.

Stedman-Edwards, Pamela
 1998   Root Causes of Biodiversity Loss: An Analytical
        Approach. Washington, DC: World Wild Fund for
        Nature.

Survival
2009 Call for Napalm Bombing of "Savages" Wins Survival Racism Award. Electronic document, http://www.survivalinternational.org/news/4885, accessed October 14, 2009.

Tello, Rodolfo
2004 Culture and Environment in the Native Community of Queros. Institutional publication, 28 pages. Cusco, Perú: Pro-Manu.

Terborgh, John
2000 The Fate of Tropical Forests: A Matter of Stewardship. Conservation Biology 14 (5): 1358–1361.
2004 [1999] Requiem for Nature. Washington, DC: Island Press.

Tucker, Bram
2001 The Behavioral Ecology and Economics of Variation, Risk, and Diversification among Mikea Forager-Farmers of Madagascar. PhD dissertation. Department of Anthropology, University of North Carolina at Chapel Hill.
2006 A Future Discounting Explanation for the Persistence of a Mixed Foraging-Horticulture Strategy among the Mikea of Madagascar. *In* Behavioral Ecology and the Transition to Agriculture. Douglas Kennett and Bruce Winterhalder, eds. Pp. 22–40. Berkeley: University of California Press.
2007 Perception of Interannual Covariation and Strategies for Risk Reduction among Mikea of Madagascar. Human Nature 18: 162–180.

Van Nieuwkoop, Martien and Jorge Uquillas
2000   Defining Ethnodevelopment in Operational Terms:
       Lessons from the Ecuador Indigenous and Afro-
       Ecuadorian Peoples Development Project. LCR
       Sustainable Development Working Paper No 6.
       Washington, DC: The World Bank.

Vayda, Andrew
2009   Explaining Human Actions and Environmental
       Changes. Lanham, MD: Altamira Press.

Vickers, William
1994   From Opportunism to Nascent Conservation: The Case
       of the Siona-Secoya. Human Nature 5 (4): 307–337.

Warren, Michael
2001   The Role of the Global Network of Indigenous
       Knowledge Resource Centers in the Conservation of
       Cultural and Biological Diversity. *In* On Biocultural
       Diversity: Linking Language, Knowledge, and the
       Environment. Luisa Maffi, ed. Pp. 446–461. Washington,
       DC: Smithsonian Institution Press.

Wilshusen, Peter, Steven Brechin, Crystal Fortwangler, and
Patrick West
2002   Reinventing a Square Wheel: Critique of a Resurgent
       "Protection Paradigm" in International Biodiversity
       Conservation. Society & Natural Resources 15: 17–40.

Wood, Alexander, Pamela Stedman-Edwards, and Johana
Mang, eds.
2000   The Root Causes of Biodiversity Loss. Sterling, VA:
       Earthscan Publications.